Together We Pray

Together We Pray

Pray Now Prayers, Devotions, Blessings
and Reflections on 'The Sound of Prayer'

Published on behalf of
THE CHURCH OF SCOTLAND
MISSION AND DISCIPLESHIP COUNCIL

SAINT ANDREW PRESS
Edinburgh

First published in 2018 by Saint Andrew Press
SAINT ANDREW PRESS
121 George Street
Edinburgh EH2 4YN

ISBN 978 0 7152 0996 7

Please note that the views expressed in *Pray Now* are those of the
individual writer and not necessarily the official view of
the Church of Scotland, which can be laid down only by the
General Assembly.

British Library Cataloguing in Publication Data
A catalogue record for this book is available from the
British Library.

It is the publisher's policy to use only papers that are natural and
recyclable and that have been manufactured from timber grown in
renewable, properly managed forests. All of the manufacturing
processes of the papers are expected to conform to the
environmental regulations of the country of origin.

Typeset by Hugh Hillyard-Parker, Edinburgh
Printed and bound in the United Kingdom by CPI Group (UK) Ltd

Contents

Outsiders

People in Power

The Psalmists

Worshippers

The Sound of Prayer

Preface

From the opening words of the book of Genesis, to the Psalms and on to the words of Jesus in the Gospels, through the various letters written to the early Church, until the book of Revelation, the Bible is full of prayers that have been breathed, hoped, sighed, longed for and very much needed. Reading them, we realise each prayer has an accent and sound of its own, depending on who is praying and what the circumstances are.

Sometimes those prayers are private and personal.
At other times they are the prayers of the community.

They are prayers for individual situations of every kind imaginable, and they are prayers too, for all sorts of national and international dilemmas that people and nations are facing.

Very quickly, you realise there is nothing and no one that prayer cannot offer the words or the silence for. Those prayers bring God's people together. They blend our voices, join our spirits, unite our hearts as together we pray and look to God for the answers we cannot, ourselves, provide.

As Christians in the 21st century, we need to practise prayer – individually and as communities of God's people. Those prayers may well take on different forms depending on where we are and what's happening around us, but looking personally, locally and globally, we have a God with whom we can share all our thoughts and concerns, our hopes, dreams, fears and joys.

Let what follows here inspire us and encourage us to pray – whatever our accent. Bless and be blessed.

RT REV SUSAN BROWN
Moderator of the General Assembly 2018

Using this Book

Come, Holy Spirit,
open to us the treasure of Thy wisdom;
feed the hungry, ransom our prisoners,
raise up the sick, comfort the faint-hearted.

~ Early Christian prayers, attributed to
St Augustine and Clement of Rome ~

Scripture is full of prayers that often come from the mouths
of people who are particularly honest with God. Sometimes
they are joyful; at other times they are laden with lament,
but all of them carry the weight of human experience that we
can recognise somewhere in our own lives and in the lives
of others.

These prayers help us to say the things we can often find
difficult to express. They show us that nothing is off limits
with God. They invite us into a conversation. They allow us
to sympathise, perhaps even empathise with the 'other',
as we consider how we would pray with them. They
encourage us to ask what we might say to God if we were
in that very situation.

Together We Pray is the theme of this edition of *Pray Now*.
The title links the book to The Church of Scotland's national
prayer initiative, but this is a book for anyone who wants to
pray. *Pray Now* is ideal for praying individually, with family or
in a small group, with a friend or in a pastoral care situation,
in a meeting or worship gathering.

The book is in two sections: the first includes meditations and
prayers, while the second contains reflections on the theme of
'The Sound of Prayer' that consider how prayer is expressed
through sound in different circumstances and environments.

In the first section there are 52 chapters arranged under seven headings, which invite us to listen to the voices of people in scripture as they pray:

- Jesus
- Apostles
- Prophets
- Outsiders
- People in Power
- Psalmists
- Worshippers

The chapters cover a broad range of writing styles, but the structure of each chapter is the same:

- Title and scripture verse
- Meditation
- Morning prayer
- Evening prayer
- Two complementary scripture readings
- Blessing

Each chapter is based on a prayer by a specific character in scripture. These are words or actions that are deeply felt, so as we read, we might consider how these prayers resonate in our own context, reflect the experience of people in our communities and point toward current events. Your response to these scriptural prayers may differ from that of our writers, so let new prayers be inspired within you as you reflect on them.

The second section of the book contains 12 reflections on 'The Sound of Prayer', exploring different aspects of how prayer might sound. Sound is malleable: shifting, moving, reflecting, impacting – and is absorbed – in response to its environment. Sound waves touch us, whether we hear them or not. Spoken, cried, sung or felt, prayers emanate from different sources, reverberating, resonating and washing over all that they encounter, revealing something new as they permeate each one of us.

What do our prayers sound like in the midst of all the other types of noise? What prayers rise up or are drowned out? Is there a distinct sound of prayer from a particular community or context? How might we begin to listen more attentively to these prayers and what might we learn from them? These are some of the questions that the authors of the articles invite you to ponder.

The section provides blank pages where you might like to make notes as you reflect on these questions.

Many of the prayers in scripture are said by men. However, the even gender balance of the Pray Now writing group, and the way we as individual readers interpret and engage with the themes and emotions expressed in these prayers, means – we believe – that barriers of gender, culture or theology can be transcended in the prayers and resources offered in this book.

PHILL MELLSTROM
Worship Development Worker
Mission and Discipleship Council

For more information, the guide *How to Pray* can be found on the Church of Scotland website at www.churchofscotland.org.uk/connect/together_we_pray/how_we_pray or phone 0131 225 5722 and ask to be put through to the Mission and Discipleship Council.

Together we pray with

JESUS

'When you are praying, do not heap up empty phrases ...'

~ Matthew 6:7 ~

The Lord's Prayer

'Pray then in this way ...'

~ Matthew 6:9 ~

Meditation

Humility.
Hopefulness.
Gratitude.
Repentance.
Forgiveness.
Trust.
The essence of prayer.

The way to the truth
in all of life.

Not always in that order.
Not always in equal amounts.
Not loud or showy.
Not wordy or wise.
Not always short and sweet.

But always heard
and always held.

Morning Prayer

Father in heaven,
Your kingdom calls me today
to make this little bit of earth
on which I stand its home.
May I be open to Your prompting,
nourished in my faith,
forgiving in my dealings with others
and equipped to face every challenge
knowing You are with me.
In Jesus' name and in the spirit
of His words I ask this.   AMEN

Evening Prayer

Father in heaven,
thank You for the 'kingdom come' moments
of today;
for stomachs and souls replenished,
for hurts healed,
for obstacles overcome,
for hopes rekindled.
And if in some way
I have played my part
in the hallowing of Your work,
then receive this prayer
as my blessing to You.
In Jesus' name.   AMEN

Scripture Readings

Matthew 6:9–13   *The Lord's Prayer*
Ephesians 3:14–17   *Rooted and grounded in love*

Blessing

May God's kingdom come
and God's will be done
and may we, through grace,
with or without words,
know the way,
show the way,
be the way.   AMEN

Hide and seek

'I thank You, Father, Lord of heaven and earth,
because You have hidden these things from the wise
and the intelligent and have revealed them to infants.'

~ Luke 10:21 ~

Meditation

Jesus loves me – this I know,
For the Bible tells me so.
Little ones to Him belong –
They are weak but He is strong.

~ Anna Bartlett Warner (1860) ~

What a delight that the pompous don't get it!
My heart soars with praise that the elite can't see!
Those looking down on us from ivory towers
think we're looking up to them,
but they can't see what we see
above and beyond them:

the God smiling as a Father
on children, who discover that trusting God
is infinitely richer than studying God;

the God who delights in hiding from the haughty,
who spend too much time counting
and too little time playing;

the God who gleefully whispers to the little ones,
'Look! Here I am! Come and let's have some adventures!'

Morning Prayer

Lord of heaven and earth,
You are my Father and I am Your child;
whatever this day may hold,
may I keep hold of that revelation throughout.

Give me the eyes to see what only You can show.
Give me the trust to believe what only You have promised.
Give me the humility to stay small enough
to behold what only the little ones may.

Help me to see and seize the opportunities today
to build Your topsy-turvy kingdom of the littlest and the least.
AMEN

Evening Prayer

Looking back over the labours that I and others have offered,
I praise You for the glimpses of You
that shone brightest in childlike trust –
those moments raised the most smiles,
stoked the most joy.

Thank You for the deepest God-moments
in humble acts rooted in taking You at Your word.
But thank You most of all, Father,
that my name is written in heaven.   AMEN

Scripture Readings

Luke 10:21–24   *Hide (God, from the haughty)*
Luke 11:9–13   *Seek (humble children find God)*

Blessing

May God open your eyes to see
all that cannot be seen except that God reveals it.
May God open your ears to hear
the pride and joy God expresses at your humility.
May God open your heart to receive
His Word, His truth, His love.   AMEN

Gethsemane

'Could you not keep awake one hour?'

~ Mark 14:37 ~

Meditation

Have we lost the fury in this moment, God?
Have we sanitised Your despair, Jesus,
simply because we know the ending is good?
Do we struggle to stay awake for one hour?
And in so doing, lose it all?
Shake us awake, God.
Open our eyes
to the disciples' betrayal
by falling asleep.
Sharpen the image in our mind's eye
to the highest definition possible.

In real time, HD, whatever makes it happen for us,
let's have the courage to see
the ultimate plea bargain
between Father and Son
and the absolute loneliness of Christ in this moment.

Let us have the courage to recognise
our own complicity in this sleepy betrayal
that says a deep resounding 'NO' to Jesus.

Let us put a stop to pressing
the snooze button on faith.
Shake us awake, God.

Morning Prayer

In the shards of dusty morning light
that pierce through the curtains of life,
let us be awake to You, O God.
Let us start this day the right way,
with You.
Let us remain with You
wherever we go, today.   AMEN

Evening Prayer

Forgive us, Lord Jesus,
when our eyes became heavy
and our focus blurred.
Forgive us for the moments
when we said 'no' to You today.
Forgive us for falling asleep in our faith.

As we close this day,
in forgiveness,
may we begin again tomorrow,
wide awake, in You.   AMEN

Scripture Readings

Mark 14:35–38   *Praying while the disciples sleep*
Psalm 130   *My soul waits for the Lord*

Blessing

May God bless you,
from the rising of the sun in the east,
to its setting in the west.   AMEN

'Father, glorify Your name'

'Father, glorify Your name.'

~ John 12:28 ~

Meditation

Bearing the blow of hearing
that each breath is a promise
of one more moment;
wrestling with the knowledge
that life is a gift
and not inevitable.
If this is to be the last of conversations,
then may words be kind
and full of the hope not felt or assumed.
If this is to be the last press of skin,
then may the tenderness
and comfort offered
bring reconciliation
and reminders of our purpose.
In the diminishing moments of life
remove the selfishness of personal need
to recognise the gift of Christ
in those who cry for justice
and those who carry love
into the tears of the world.

Morning Prayer

Father,
may Your name be glorified
this day,
in well-intentioned words and actions;
may I notice
Your glory
when I fail to speak of love,
or to be the bearer of justice to another.

Let me remember
that Your gift of life
is bigger than my presence and life,
and more encompassing
of the creation
of which I am but a part.   AMEN

Evening Prayer

It was not me who spoke with tenderness
and revealed love.
It was not me who carried hope into a room
and brought light.
It was not me who offered a hand to hold
and gifted strength.
Yet in these,
and any activity made in Christ's name,
Your Spirit is revealed,
Dancing Creator,
and the glory of God enters time and space
to greet the need of the world.   AMEN

Scripture Readings

John 12:27–36   *Jesus speaks about His death*
Matthew 5:15–16   *Allowing our light to shine*

Blessing

Glory to Your name
as the Creator's purpose is lived by those who care.
Glory to Your name
as the Son's life brings light to those who follow.
Glory to Your name
as the Spirit's impetus inspires changed living.
AMEN

Before raising Lazarus

'Father, I thank You for having heard me. I knew that You
always hear me, but I have said this for the sake of the crowd
standing here, so that they may believe that You sent me.'

~ John 11:41–42 ~

Meditation

Mary knelt at His feet
(the posture of the spiritual life),
Martha believed in the resurrection
(the power of God one day),
but Lazarus, without speech,
– unable to speak? –
clouded the eyes of Jesus and
shone with Eternity.

The cave a womb,
the stone a suggestion that
the Lord is in this place, and
if we dare to close our eyes,
enter the still darkness of prayer,
of faith and of God,
we will see immortality;
eternity born in us.

Jesus is not immortal
because He was raised;
He was raised
because He is immortal.
Immortality is now,
He told Martha.
Do you see?

Morning Prayer

In a universe of ten dimensions or more,
in a cosmos of miraculous complexity,
in a creation that is beautiful and mysterious,

let me see that, with imagination and intuition,
I may encounter the Holy.
Through the wonders of science
and the wonders for which science has no words,
through the dimensions of scripture,
its poetry, mythology and spirituality,
let me see the One that eyes cannot see.
The *Shekinah** is at home within me;
my soul is filled with the essence of Eternity:
Christ within me.   AMEN

Evening Prayer

Infinite God
– two words, together and separately,
that we cannot comprehend,
confined always by the mind's possibilities –
grant me Your peace beyond understanding.
Like Mary, may I sit at the feet of Jesus
and ponder His call in my heart.
I crave intimacy with You:
be born in me.   AMEN

Scripture Readings

John 11:30–44   *Blindness, sight and immortality*
John 9:13–25   *Sight and inner sight*

Blessing

Close my eyes, O God,
to distractions,
to pious words;
sensitise my soul's perception,
enlarge my awareness of You:
let me live in You and You in me,
at one, tasting immortality. AMEN

**in Hebrew, the dwelling-place of God
or the divine presence of God*

Crying out

'My God, my God, why have You forsaken me?'

~ Mark 15:34 ~

Meditation

From a place deep within
I give voice to what I fear.

Opening my mouth,
waiting for the sound to come –
letting go
of all I have held back.

Why? Why? WHY?
The question sounds like an echo
in my soul.

Yet in asking, I find release.
Crying out, being heard,
I am one with Him.

Morning Prayer

My voice rises to You O God,
silently, softly,
knowing You are there.

Before I name You,
You are present.
Before I call on You,
You are answering.

Praise be to the One,
Who has given me voice.

In the hours ahead,
let my words be considered –
rooted in Your own wisdom.

Let my questions feed
both searching and learning.

Every day is new with You.   AMEN

Evening Prayer

There are moments each day
that lead to questions and doubt.
Remind me God,
You are in all I experience.

I cry out to You,
and seek Your peace this night.

Let me cry out with Christ
and with all who voice
pain and distress.
in humanity and humility.
We are united in You.

My God, my God,
in darkness and light
let me know You have not forsaken me.
You are always there.   AMEN

Scripture Readings

> Mark 15:25–39   *Crying out*
> Psalm 22:1–5   *Being heard*

Blessing

> May the God who gives life and breath
> also give you voice –
> to praise, to pray,
> to cry out,
> with confidence.   AMEN

Last shout

'Father, into Your hands I commend My spirit.'
~ Luke 23:46 ~

Meditation

Into Your hands...
Your known hands,
Your gentle hands,
Your strong hands,
hands that are trustworthy,
hands that sculpted galaxies and brushed grasses in the garden,
hands that handle hot coals and wipe away tears,
hands that will catch me,
hands that will release me.

I commend my spirit ...
I hand over my essence and my energy,
the best of me,
the worst of me,
and the in-between,
which is most of me.
I entrust myself,
I turn myself in,
I pour myself out,
knowing there is nothing left, and this is my last gasp,
and consciousness is fading, and the flame is sputtering,
and in the end,
You are.

Morning Prayer

Oh God,
if only I could commend all my dying into Your hands ...
the moments when I'm dying of shame or of boredom,
dreams that hit the dust and splinter,
hope that curls up and withers,
the loss of what I have loved.

Can I place it all in Your safekeeping?
Today, will You help me when that valley must be walked?
No foreboding wall has power to cut me off from You.
Keep close, faithful God,
through whatever ends and is no more.
Console me again with what will never die –
Your irrepressible love.
So be it! AMEN

Evening Prayer

Tonight, Lord God,
will You catch the ones whose dying shout goes unheard,
whose last breath is premature,
who should have seen tomorrow?
Will You cradle the ones who fall asleep in peace,
whose bedside has been a place of vigil,
whose hands are held in the crossing over?
Will You stay where death is a welcomed friend,
a despised victor,
an accepted attender,
a normality?
You receive us at our endings;
into Your care we fall and rest and live again.
This we know through Jesus
who has been there. AMEN

Scripture Readings

Luke 23:44–49 *Jesus' final cry from the cross*
Romans 14:7–9 *Living or dying, we are the Lord's*

Blessing

May God the Omega bless us
in all our letting go,
in all our giving over,
in all that is finished. AMEN

Together we pray with

THE APOSTLES

Think of us in this way, as servants of Christ and stewards of God's mysteries.

~ 1 Corinthians 4:1 ~

Peace be to the whole community

Peace be to the whole community, and love with faith,
from God the Father and the Lord Jesus Christ.

~ Ephesians 6:23 ~

Meditation

I bind unto myself today
the cloak of all embracing love
and the strong shoes of practical power.

> May my cloak and my shoes,
> reflect the love and power
> planted deeply within by the source of all light,
> to strengthen, affirm and heal
> the whole community.

I bind unto myself today
the hat of many options
and the stole of compassion.

> May I have the wisdom to reach deep
> into the hat when a conundrum presents itself,
> and the humility to seek replenishment from others.
> May I have the grace to wrap the stole of compassion
> around those within the community who hurt.

I bind unto myself today
the feather boa of light-heartedness
and the tickling stick of delight.

> In the face of overwhelming need and hurt,
> – and only when the time is right –
> may this community find laughter and joy
> in all of God's good creation.

Morning Prayer

Dear Lord, as I arise this day, may I put on
the cloak of Your love,
the power of Your shoes,
the wisdom of Your hat,
the peace of Your prayer stole,
to equip me for all that I do, with all whom I meet,
and so to extend the reach
of Your love, power and wisdom
through the whole community.   AMEN

Evening Prayer

As I take my rest, I give thanks for this day.
As I lay down my garments of peace,
so refresh me dear Lord,
that tomorrow I may be ready, clothed
to nurture Your peace in the whole community.   AMEN

Scripture Readings

Ephesians 6:10–24   *Peace be to the whole community*
John 14:27   *'My peace I give to you'*

Blessing

May the blessing of the God of peace
encircle you,
your community,
and all whom you love,
today and always.   AMEN

When we fall

He fell to the ground three floors below.

~ Acts 20:9 ~

Meditation

Ios, Ayia Napa, Santorini, Malia, Mykonos –
the hottest party destinations in the Med.
A whole year of saving up
for a week with the lads.
Lifelong friends – memories to last a lifetime.
That had been the plan
until my best friend, Euan – all the way from primary one –
fell to the ground three floors below
and was picked up dead.

I don't know what happened.
None of us do.
We wish we did;
we wish we could explain;
we wish there was something we could have done.
We were invincible
until the moment
we were not.

'His life is in him,' said the minister, back home.
I don't really understand,
but in a way, I do.
We thought we were invincible –
and maybe we are, in a different way.
Maybe Euan's life is in him,
just like Eutychus.
Maybe God, maybe.

Morning Prayer

Lord God, we pray for the families
that suffer the tragedy of a life cut short.
We pray for all those involved in picking up the pieces,
reaching out when life falls apart.
For those unthinkable moments,
we pause to reflect
and ask for Your love and peace.   AMEN

Evening Prayer

Let us pray tonight
for all who work to keep us safe
when the night is young and the party goes on.
We remember the work of those who pastor in the streets,
seeking to strengthen community in Christ's name.
Help them to listen, care and help,
especially when it is needed most.   AMEN

Scripture Readings

Acts 20:7–12   *Prayer for young man falling out of
a window*
Psalm 145:14–19   *God lifts the fallen*

Blessing

When the party is in full swing, may God be with us.
When we are invincible, may God be with us.
When we fall, may God be with us.
May God be the life in us – no matter what.   AMEN

Seeing with the heart

The eyes of your heart enlightened.

~ Ephesians 1:18 ~

Meditation

Wherein lies the heart of your faith?
In the beauty of a sanctuary?
In the glories of the world of nature?
In the treasury of scripture unlocked?
In the believing that turns from seeing and
thinking to doing and following?

Where are the veils of unknowing heaviest?
Is mystery a wilful cloak for ignorance?
Does the search for truth blind us to
the need for wonder?

When faith seeks understanding,
is there room in our heart and eyes
for the threads of light and shade,
colour and grey that provide the texture
of belief?

And after the searching and questioning,
the waiting and comprehending,
does God's dynamic Spirit propel
our faith into deeds of mercy, joy and love?

Morning Prayer

Lord,
in the dawning of this new day,
framed with intentions of outstretched hours,
shape my mind, that it may be clear but not closed;
shape my hands, that they may be open and not clenched;
shape my mouth, that it may be generous and not sour;
shape my feet, that they may be deliberate and not wayward;

shape my heart, that it may be loving and not hateful.
And so enlightened, may I serve Christ and His world.
AMEN

Evening Prayer

Present God,
as into sleep I drift,
I lay me down the weight of this day,
its worries and cares,
its successes and failures,
its quickness and slowness.
I give myself, known and unknown,
conscious and unconscious,
into the hands of my merciful Saviour.
Where I have brought light, and lifted darkness,
let blessing follow.
Where I have brought darkness, and shut off light,
let grace come soon that I may try again
to see with Your heart the opportunities I have missed.
In Jesus' Name.   AMEN

Scripture Readings

Exodus 10:12–21   *The heart in action*
Ephesians 1:17–19   *Seeing with your heart*

Blessing

In what you see, may you find wisdom;
in what you hear, may you find gentleness;
in what you feel, may you find compassion;
in what you smell, may you find sanctity;
in what you taste, may you find flavour;
and in what you believe, may you find
the sense and presence of Christ.   AMEN

The riches of God's glory

*I pray that, according to the riches of His glory, He
may grant that you may be strengthened in your inner
being with power through His Spirit.*

~ Ephesians 3:16 ~

Meditation

The congregation gathers
and through the vestry door
the hubbub of the morning
breaks the silence.
The choir melody of final rehearsal
offers moments of discord and harmony,
recalling moments of a week
spent in service of the living Christ.
The whispered tones of individuals sharing news
both buoyant
and heartbreaking,
offering signs of the Spirit at work.
These saints rumble with the heights and depths
of the richness of the Lord.
Their individual lives
bring colour and hue,
pace and energy
to what it means to live as Christ's people.
Their prayers shared in word and silence
listen for heaven's thoughts,
and offer echoes of the relationship
with the Eternal One.

Morning Prayer

Glory to the Lord of the morning,
who has awoken us
to the experience of life
shared with the Holy Spirit.

We pray for all that this day holds,
whether it be tears or laughter,
stillness or activity.
May Christ walk with us
and settle in our conversations and tasks,
that love may ooze from every pore.   AMEN

Evening Prayer

In the thrills of this day,
You, Companion of Life, were there,
sharing the laughter,
hoping for the best,
sensing the friendship.
In the sorrow of this day,
You were there,
Comforting Presence,
easing the anger,
feeding the hunger,
holding the hurt.
In the silence of the night,
may we find our restoration in You
as You prepare us
for all a new day will bring.   AMEN

Scripture Readings

Ephesians 3:14–19   *The riches of God's glory*
1 Timothy 2:1–7   *Instructions concerning prayer*

Blessing

Glory,
to the Lord who brings blessing to each day;
to the Christ who brings blessing to God's people;
to the Holy Spirit who brings blessing to creativity.
AMEN

What is best

That Your love may overflow more and more.

~ Philippians 1:9 ~

Meditation

Good. Better. Best.
I can guess what stage I'm at.
Overflowing with love –
a little too demanding.
Pure and blameless –
in my dreams.
Knowledge and insight –
I wish.
But there is time.
For love never runs out,
even if it doesn't always flow out of me.
There is wisdom in the face of ignorance.
There is vision despite blindness.
There is perfection regardless of flaw.
There is a promise
of the best yet to come.

Morning Prayer

If this prayer
could make me perfect, Lord,
or equip me with the answer
to every question I may face today
then my harvest might be plentiful.
But all You ask is that I love, and love,
and love even more.
Help me then to be loving today,
of You and others
that I might come a little closer
to what You seek of me.
In Jesus' name.   AMEN

Evening Prayer

Thank You, Lord
for the harvest of today.
For the kind words,
the generous gestures,
the goodness in among
the not so good.
And thank You
for the gentle reminders
that You know me best of all.
This is my prayer.   AMEN

Scripture Readings

Philippians 1:9–11   *What is best*
Psalm 37:5   *Trust in God*

Blessing

In our asking,
in our serving,
in our seeking,
may we be grounded,
may we be guided,
may we be graced,
with love.   AMEN

Wellbeing

I pray that all may go well with you.

~ 3 John 2 ~

Meditation

Is all well with my soul?
It's not a question I stop to think about often.
Is all well with my soul?
Perhaps I should pause and consider.

A deep breath,
a quiet space,
a chance to be.

God,
is all well with my soul?

I hear God:
'Are you thriving?'
'Are you living life to the full?'
'For I have come, that you may have life;
receive it as My gift.'

My soul rests in You, O God,
You are my salvation.

Morning Prayer

Centre and Source,
You are always living and breathing,
painting the landscape
and announcing a new day with You.

In You, I find my strength and song;
in You, I celebrate all that is good and well;
in You, I place my trust.
You know me more than I know myself.

Let my prayer rise to You,
and with it my open heart and mind,
to know and love You
always more.   AMEN

Evening Prayer

I give thanks to You, God,
for all that is well within me.
I give thanks for all Your goodness –
the gifts I received today.

Help me rest in Your truth
renewed by Your strength.
You sustain and guide me
and surprise me too.

As I recognise my own needs,
I pray too, for all who are troubled
in body, mind and spirit.
I trust You are always faithful.

I praise You for who I am,
and who You call me to become.   AMEN

Scripture Readings

3 John 1–8   *Wellbeing*
Deuteronomy 30:15–20   *Choose life*

Blessing

The blessing of the God of life;
the blessing of the Christ of love;
the blessing of the Spirit of peace;
always.   AMEN

Held fast

Into an inheritance that is imperishable, undefiled,
and unfading, kept in heaven for you.

~ 1 Peter 1:4 ~

Meditation

When life is filled with contradictions and paradoxes;
distress, threats, trials and testing.
When we fear faith will fail ...

Disorientated! Shaken!
Yet we are assured ...
Christ will hold us fast.

The way of Jesus is the path of suffering and glory;
as God's chosen strangers,
we live amidst paradox and contradiction.
Yet we are assured ...
Christ will hold us fast.

Faith finds home 'in Christ',
reassurance
that Christ is the anchor of our souls;
that we are not forgotten.
Christ –
preserving, keeping and guarding us.
This our imperishable and living hope.

Christ will hold us fast.

Morning Prayer

I approach this day expectantly,
trusting in the fullness of Your mercy and grace,
no matter the path before me.
I look to You for reassurance,
as the One to preserve, keep and guard
my life and my faith –

to hold me fast in Your keeping
throughout this day.
In Jesus' name.   AMEN

Evening Prayer

In You, heavenly Father,
we find refuge and strength.
In You, Christ,
we are rescued and restored.
In You, Holy Spirit,
we are overwhelmed by amazing grace.
You clothe us,
and above all You wrap us and embrace us
in Your love.

At the close of this day
I trust and rest in these good things,
assured that I am Your child.   AMEN

Scripture Readings

1 Peter 1:1–9   *A living hope*
2 Corinthians 1:3–11   *Consolation in hard times*

Blessing

May the faithfulness and promises of God
hold you fast in every circumstance,
overwhelm you with grace and
grant you a secure hope for the future.   AMEN

Together we pray with

THE PROPHETS

Speak, Lord, for Your servant is listening.

~ 1 Samuel 3:9 ~

'Let it be known this day'

'O Lord, God of Abraham, Isaac, and Israel, let it be known
this day that you are God in Israel, that I am your servant,
and that I have done all these things at your bidding.'

~ 1 Kings 18:36 ~

Meditation

It wasn't in the preaching or the power or the prideful victory.
It wasn't in the warring words or the targeted threats
or the full-on fear.
It wasn't in the righteous certainty or the bold, brash clatter.
It was in the fragile 'I'm sorry', in the proffered peace.

It was in the waiting and the walking,
the deep listening and the tumultuous travel
from heavily defended corners to common ground.
It was in the journey, the justice, the entwined hands,
and the outstretched arms and the wide-open welcome.
It was in the stillness and the soft embrace,
the sheer silence and the standing together in it.

It was and is and will be in longed-for love,
in the Divine's ardent prayer for peace,
and in humanity's heart and ear,
swept up in the all-consuming fire of justice,
and in that still small voice
that calls us towards each other.

Morning Prayer

In the hectic churn of day to day,
we rarely reflect on where we've been,
much less take a breath at break of day
to imagine where we want to go.
Breathe now,
and let the Divine design a day with you:

May it be known that on this day
I stole time with my lover;
I played with the children
and became one of them for a glorious moment;
I found a new friend by slowing down with a stranger;
and cherished those old comfortable friends
who are familiar as cosy furniture.

Let it be known this day
because it is shown in how I live this day.   AMEN

Evening Prayer

In the embers of evening,
heart back to still,
mind back to calm,
body, lay me down tonight.

Spirit, restless and wild for justice;
Spirit, passionate for peace;
Spirit, ceaselessly searching for unity;
keep me ever awake to the world You dream,
as I lay me down this night.   AMEN

Scripture Readings

1 Kings 18:36–41   *'Let it be known this day'*
Amos 5:21–24   *Justice and righteousness*

Blessing

Blessed be the strident and the still.
Blessed be the protest and the peace.
Blessed be the voice and the vacuum.
Blessed be all the twists and turnings that bring us
home to You.   AMEN

Balance of power

Then Elisha prayed: 'O Lord, please open his eyes that
he may see.' So the Lord opened the eyes of the
servant, and he saw; the mountain was full of horses
and chariots of fire all around Elisha.

~ 2 Kings 6:17 ~

Meditation

Angels, shape shifted into chargers,
snorting fire, ready for the jokes of God.
Angels, seldom hidden from the wise,
smiling peace, calming all our fear-filled croaks.
Angels, serving unseen plans of faith and love,
without whose work the spokes of life would crack.

Faith sees the invisible,
'a spirit of wisdom and revelation',
as Paul once prayed,
to see things as they really are,
with Jesus raised from death and ruling over all things.
We do not yet see this physically, but 'we see Jesus',
and that is something more than even an army of angels.

Sometimes awfulness unfolds with no end in sight;
at other times the marvellous lifts us where we stand.

Morning Prayer

Lord God, grant me double vision:
to see Your image in unlikely people;
to see Your hand in difficult circumstances;
to see Your feet set down upon our troubled world;
to see Your will take shape somewhere within my life today.

But grant me too that single mind
that trusts Your goodness even when my sight is weak,
that single heart that does the work of faith
no matter who is tempting me.

Through Jesus Christ,
who knew that things unseen were all-important.   AMEN

Evening Prayer

It is time for me to see You, God invisible.
It is time for me to touch You, God unformed.
It is time for me to hear You speaking to my heart,
It is time for me to grasp You with the hands and eyes of faith.

Lord, sometimes my life seems written in poetry,
and I feel the highs and lows.
Sometimes my life is prose,
a life I just get on and deal with.

Whoever I am, You know my waking and my sleeping,
You saw me growing in my mother's womb,
and You will see me home,
as You did Your Son, our Saviour, Jesus Christ.   AMEN

Scripture Readings

| 2 Kings 6:15–23 | *The balance of power* |
| Ephesians 1:15–23 | *The power of prayer* |

Blessing

May the God beyond sight
   open wide your eyes to God's beauty;
the God beyond stars
   open wide your world to God's presence;
the God beyond thought
   open wide your thinking mind;
the God beyond words
   open wide your listening ears.
May your life be balanced in God's powerful palm.
AMEN

The land mourns

'How long will the land mourn,
and the grass of every field wither?'

~ Jeremiah 12:4 ~

Meditation

How long will the land mourn,
shifting, sighing, lowing,
in the midst of all that has been done?
For how long will flowers blossom –
tears upon the cheeks of dry earth?
For how long will the laughter lines
of rocky ridges ring
with the hope of new days?
For how long?
How many more mercenaries will profit
from the earth's loss?

Why do so many jealously guard
what is freely given?
Why do so many hoard
what is limitless?
How do they justify their actions?
With what accounts? With what records?
Where is the earth's ledger?
Why have so many borrowed so much
on our behalf?
Our only collateral our home.
Why is our reckoning not theirs?
Why is shame so profitable?
And dignity without market value?
Why? How? For how long?

Morning Prayer

Creator of all land and all people,
we bring before You our concerns, fears and worries
for the earth
– our home
and livelihood.
We ask for opportunities
to heal,
to restore,
to cherish
the earth on which we walk.   AMEN

Evening Prayer

Patient Saviour,
we thank You that You listen
to our complaints
and our cries,
both eloquent
and incomprehensible.
Thank You for sending Your spirit
to advocate for us wordlessly,
interceding for us this day
with sighs too deep for words.   AMEN

Scripture Readings

Jeremiah 12:1–4   *How long will the land mourn?*
Romans 8:26–30   *Sighs too deep for words*

Blessing

Bless our land with fresh flowing water
and bless our leaders with fresh flowing humility,
honesty
and courage.   AMEN

The searing word

Unclean lips ...

~ Isaiah 6:5 ~

Meditation

In a world drowning in words,
sift through what you say.
Do your words bring weal or woe,
and is there purpose?
Do your words bring healing or hurt,
and is there cause?
Do your words offer praise, or pain,
and is there need?

God calls God's children
to speak truth in love,
to utter kindness in the time of despair,
and to understand that words in themselves
have the power to create and to destroy.

In Jesus we have the Word of Life,
Whose words brought challenge and forgiveness,
questioning and answering,
health and hopefulness,
into His world.
He spoke into silence and storm,
and let His words create ripples of light and mercy
in lives where speech had harmed or held back.

Speak well this day.

Morning Prayer

Lord Jesus Christ,
living Word of God,
when I open my mouth today,
before I speak, let me look;
before I speak, let me listen;

before I speak, let me understand;
so that when I speak, my weighed words
might not be a burden but a blessing,
and say something that is needed.
Let my lips be clean,
and my words spring from a pure heart.
For Jesus' sake. AMEN

Evening Prayer

Gracious God,
let the words of this day fall silent:
the kind words that have encouraged me;
the cruel words that have corroded me;
the pointless words that have emptied me;
the powerful words that have uplifted me.
Into the speechless night,
and in the gentle silence,
let Your unspoken words of kindness and rest
enfold me now in blessing,
and with me this word-weary world.

Word of Life, I pray that in this stillness,
new strength may come
and sentences of love be formed to fill
the day that is to come.
In Jesus' name. AMEN

Scripture Readings

Isaiah 6:1–8   *The searing word*
James 3:1–12   *The tongue is a fire*

Blessing

Word of Life,
heal, forgive,
comfort, bless.
Be still, be glad,
and be at peace. AMEN

Courageous prayer

*Daniel got down on his knees three times a day to pray
to his God and praise Him, just as he had done
previously.*

~ Daniel 6:10 ~

Meditation

God the Creator, I kneel to You.
In awe I bend low and offer
prayers of gratitude; songs of praise,
as I have done all my days.

> As I look into the eyes of my oppressors
> and face forces set to destroy and kill,
> I pray for courage.

God the Son I kneel to You,
seeking forgiveness
for all evil, hardship and harm
in our world.

> As I notice in my enemies hints of my own failings,
> and face inner forces of doubt,
> I pray for forgiveness.

God the Spirit I kneel to You.
Encircle with compassion,
kindness and delight,
all those who seek to destroy.

> As I smell in my enemies rank hatred and fear
> and confess my own portion of hatred,
> I pray for compassion.

Three-in-one, living God, I kneel before You
in the rhythm of my day,
morning, noon and night
bowing low, seeking courage.

Morning Prayer

With all those facing fear, terror or uncertainty,
we pray for the courage of Daniel.
May we, with him, find,
in the rhythm of the day
and the pattern of prayer,
Your solace and Your comfort
compassionate Lord.   AMEN

Evening Prayer

We lay before You,
dear, all-embracing Jesus,
those imprisoned, persecuted,
or living in fear of their lives,
because of the prayers they utter.

And we pray for those
who live and act out of fear-filled hatred.
May they experience a radical reformation:
a transformation
of head, heart, sight and action
that brings love within, and peace without.   AMEN

Scripture Readings

Daniel 6	*Courageous prayer*
Matthew 4:1–11	*In the wilderness*

Blessing

A blessing of the God of courage be yours.
A blessing of the God of compassion be yours.
A blessing of the triune God, Creator, Son and Spirit
be yours, now and always.   AMEN

Enough

*Elijah went a day's journey into the wilderness… and
asked that he might die: 'It is enough; now, O Lord.'*

~ 1 Kings 19:4 ~

Meditation

Silent despair!
Despondency descended
like a thick blanketing fog,
threatening to suffocate.
Companion of sadness, melancholy, despair and apathy.
Tears my bread, day and night!

Despondency.
A restlessness of soul.
Faith disintegrates. Fear overwhelms.
Loss of joy and trust in God.
Resistance to love for God or neighbour.
Forsakenness that hardens the heart.

Enough!

Led deep into the wilderness,
a place of desolation and solitude,
to the place of encounter.
In this hiding place,
out of the silence,
God's hand brings restful reassurance.
A word is spoken:

'Arise!'

Nourishment for the journey ahead.
In time …
Restored, re-called and sent.

Morning Prayer

Look at me and see me in my darkness.
Hear me and listen to me in my despair.
When my soul is tormented, cast down, restless ...
When even faith seems to drift away.
I say, 'Enough Lord!'

Come to me and meet me here.
Chase away those things that cause me such sorrow.
Lift me out of the darkness and despair of this wilderness.
Speak to me and show me Your way.
Restore Your joy to me that I may serve You.   Amen

Evening Prayer

Those who are bent by the wind shall rise again
when the wind softens. (Te Whiti of Parihaka)

As the day closes, I cease all my strivings.
Lord, liberate me from my noise and chaos – quieten my soul.
Bottle up the flood of my tears – comfort my soul.
Throughout this night be present with me.
Flood my heart with deep peace
and with the light of Your way.
And as the wind softens,
speak Your truths into the silence of my heart.   Amen

Scripture Readings

1 Kings 19:1–18   *In the wilderness*
Psalm 43   *Hope in God*

Blessing

The fullness of God,
Father, Son and Holy Spirit,
meet you and satisfy you
with deep peace and ineffable joy.   Amen

From the depths of hell

'I called to the Lord out of my distress
and He answered me;
out of the belly of Sheol I cried,
and You heard my voice.'

~ Jonah 2:1 ~

Meditation

I was done.
Overwhelmed, submerged, a ton of pressure on top of me,
descending deeper and darker,
I could not find my way up.

Swirling, swooning, sweating.
Drowning, dreading, dropping.
I hit rock bottom.
How did I get here?
How did it happen so fast?

I'm still here in this hell.
Still in the depths with no strength to rise.
Yet the miracle is – I'm still here.

The Lord has preserved me –
a quiet place of waiting in the belly of the beast.

A little hope stirs that there's a reason for it;
that God will lift me out of this; that
I am not done.

Morning Prayer

As I rise today, I have not yet surfaced.
Waking just makes me conscious
that my head is not yet above water.
Lift me, O Lord! Deliver me from hell!
Trouble the waters with saving might
that I may breathe in great free gulps of air.

Today, I choose to cling to You, Lord God.
There's nothing else to cling to that can lift me from the depths.
There's no one else to cling to that can give the grace I need.
You alone can lift me, save me,
set my feet firmly on the ground once again.   AMEN

Evening Prayer

I am still here.
And You, Lord – You have been there the whole time:
when it felt as if I was alone;
when it seemed as though You'd abandoned me;
when I yearned and stretched, then faded and folded.
You were there.

From dawn to dusk,
up high You have called me and down low You have lifted me.
Even in the cold quiet of night,
You don't let the darkness consume me.

I will give You thanks,
for when I called to You from the depths of hell,
even there You came to lead me out.
I will rest in the hope that You're leading me
somewhere better.   AMEN

Scripture Readings

Jonah 2:1–9   *Deliver me from hell*
Psalm 77   *When powerless, remember God's power*

Blessing

God give you shelter from the storm,
but when you are thrown over by the storms,
may you rejoice to survive by God's grace.

God lift you from the deepest pit,
but when you are lifted to the surface,
may you rejoice to thrive in God's service.   AMEN

Dance of deliverance

'Sing to the Lord, for He has triumphed gloriously.'

~ Exodus 15:21 ~

Meditation

Shooka *cha*ka, shooka *cha*ka,
shooka *cha*ka, shooka *cha*ka,
Shooka *cha*ka, shooka *cha*ka,
shooka *cha*ka, shooka *cha*!

See the sisters go out singing
with a tambourine a-ringing,
thanks to God they are a-bringing
with their dancing bodies swinging.
In the breeze their hair a-blowing,
joyful leaps with arms a-throwing,
like a wave their bodies flowing,
feet in rhythm, faces glowing.

See the prophetess ecstatic
after army chase traumatic
she's become a praise fanatic
making gratitude emphatic.
Hear what Miriam's expressing,
thanking God for awesome blessing,
in the hour of need, no messing,
ending years of harsh oppressing.

Now the women, celebrating
the release they were awaiting,
in their dance communicating
God's most gracious vindicating.
Highest praises that they can sing
have no better voice than dancing!
Highest praises that they can sing
have no better voice than dancing!

Morning Prayer

God of Miriam and Moses,
let this be a day of dancing!
Yes, a day to move, to sing,
to let my body do the praying.
Barefoot,
bowed down,
running,
reaching up,
playing spoons,
howling at the moon.
Let me find the music and the moving
that gets past all the words and lets me tell You how it is.
Graceful God,
shall we dance?   AMEN!

Evening Prayer

O God, deliver us from evil,
from inertia,
from passivity,
from sedentary living.
Would that Your church might dance again.
Thank You for our sisters and brothers in Christ
who have never forgotten how.   AMEN

Scripture Readings

Exodus 15:1–21   *Singing of God's saving power*
Jeremiah 31:1–14   *Rejoice in the dance*

Blessing

May God who moves mountains
move us onto the floor.   AMEN

Together we pray with

OUTSIDERS

*For I am convinced that neither death, nor life,
nor angels, nor rulers, nor things present,
nor things to come, nor powers, nor height,
nor depth, nor anything else in all creation,
will be able to separate us from the love of God.*

~ Romans 8:38–39 ~

Yearning for God

Anna ... never left the temple but worshipped there
with fasting and prayer night and day.

~ Luke 2:36–37 ~

Meditation

A servant with a burning hope.
Withdrawn to the solitary place,
the place of sanctuary,
the holy place.
Yearning for God day and night,
anchored and rooted in the house of prayer,
filled with reverent awe,
fasting and praying without ceasing.

Little noticed on the margins,
insignificant.
A shadow among others,
lowly,
filled with humility and grace.
Faithfully waiting, trusting, anticipating.
Patiently looking forward
with perseverance in faith.
Life grounded in the promises of God.

Then the moment.
Welcoming the revelation of God.
The awe and wonder, delighting in Him – the Messiah.
The unspeakable joy,
overflowing.
Telling of the Child who is freedom!

Morning Prayer

With my hands cupped,
I wait to receive all You will grant me in this day.
Give me Yourself for You are all I need.

With hands reaching up and open
to the coming of Your presence,
allow me to see glimpses of where You are present in this day.

With hands extended and palms open,
enable me to accept in love and with grace
all that unfolds today.

With hands ready to work, Lord,
I am willing to serve You,
attending to what You will and purpose.
In my yearning, keep my heart steadfast in You.   AMEN

Evening Prayer

I offer up to You Lord,
the thankfulness for all I have received in this day,
the joy of glimpses of where You have been present,
the cherishing of all that unfolded.

My deep yearning for You
has not strayed.
I remain Yours.
Keep watch over me in the night.   AMEN

Scripture Readings

Luke 2:36–38   *Yearning for God*
Hebrews 12:1–3   *Run the race with perseverance*

Blessing

Await the coming of God to you.
Allow the revelation of God to sustain you.
Accept the fullness of God's glory upon you.
Attend to God's presence with hope and joy.   AMEN

The Syrian woman

But she answered Him, 'Sir, even the dogs under the
table eat the children's crumbs.'

~ Mark 7:28 ~

Meditation

Were the disciples present when this discussion took place?
Or did You tell them about it later?
So many questions I'd like to ask You, Lord.
Why did You go to Syria – away from home –
and why did You not want anyone to know where You were?
Perhaps You were just exhausted. I know You were human.
Was it because they rejected You in Nazareth,
or because of all the controversy with the establishment,
or the crowds following You everywhere,
or were You still grieving over Your cousin's death?

And did You really not want to heal the woman's daughter,
because she wasn't Jewish?
You don't usually turn people away.
Wasn't 'dog' a bit harsh, or were You joking?

But You did heal the girl, even though You never saw her.
Did that unknown foreign woman persuade You
that salvation is not just for Your own people,
but for the whole world? For Gentiles as well as Jews?
For those on the outside as well as those on the inside?
So I'm included too?
Was that the turning point for You?

Morning Prayer

For sleep in the night, Lord, I praise You;
for waking me this day, I praise You.
Resting and working, may every moment be
prayerful, that by Your grace I may see You in nature,
and in every friend and stranger I meet.
In Jesus' name. AMEN

Evening Prayer

I thank You, Lord,
for the good things of this day;
may they be used for Your glory.
Forgive me Lord,
when Your redeeming and healing work was undone.
May there be less of me, and more of You,
less of my kingdom, and more of Your kingdom.
Teach me to be silent; teach me to listen;
teach me to pray; teach me to change.
Teach me to hear the cries of parents for their children,
that together we may
be drawn closer to You,
in our acts of compassion,
in trust and obedience,
in mercy and in peace.
In Jesus' name.   AMEN

Scripture Readings

Mark 7:24–30   *Healing in a foreign land*
Matthew 25:31–46   *'When was it that we saw You?'*

Blessing

Lord, may Your blessing be upon us,
on those whom we love;
on those whom we don't love;
on those who don't love us.

May Your blessings abound,
that we might all be forgiven and healed,
and all the earth cry 'Glory to God!'

Into the mother love of the Father God
we commit ourselves,
body and soul,
for time and eternity.
In Jesus' name.   AMEN

Guidance from an angel

*'O Lord, I pray, let the man of God whom You sent
come to us again and teach us what we are to do
concerning the boy who will be born.'*

~ Judges 13:8 ~

Meditation

Teach us what we are to do concerning
the child who will be born, brand new to the planet;
the stranger stepping into the sea of unfamiliar;
the idea, new and nebulous and in need of nurture;
the decision dominating our thoughts,
yet refusing to settle.

Teach us what we are to do concerning
them or us, need or want, mine or ours, now or later;
overload apathy, affluenza, fake news;
ego-mania and crippling insecurity –
diseases incubated in a chasm of inequality.

Let the One of God whom You sent come to us again
and teach us what we are to do.
Come again and teach us about the vine and the branches,
the narrow way wide with love,
about losing your life and gaining everything.
Come again and teach us about forgiving seven times seventy,
loving our enemies and our neighbours as ourselves.
Come again and tell us about the good Samaritan,
the prodigal son and the rich young ruler.

Remind us of Mother Mary, whose yes gave birth to love,
of the woman at the well and the women at the tomb.
Tell us about the sheep and the goats,
the lion and the lamb,
and how children lead the way to the kingdom of God.
Your life taught us what we are to do.
Remind us again.

Morning Prayer

As the new day dawns,
as first light spills across morning
and gives me a glimpse of a
future yet unborn,
may there be born in me
a desire for more than me.   AMEN

Evening Prayer

Guide us to sleep.
Guard us above, below, beside.
Encircle us.

Come to us in our dreaming.
Come to us in our waking.
Come to us in our living.
Come to us in our dying.

Guide us above, below, beside.
Encircle us.   AMEN

Scripture Readings

Judges 13:8–18   *Guidance from an angel*
Proverbs 8:1–7   *Wisdom calls*

Blessing

One, born of God,
Bless the hope born through us.
Bless the children born to us.
Bless the love born in us.   AMEN

Blessings to be discovered

As you have dealt with me ...

~ Ruth 1:8 ~

Meditation

There is blessing to be discovered
in the parting of the ways.
In loss, there is a finding;
in leaving, there is an arrival;
in surrender, there is a saving.
And we may find ourselves
richly hallowed in new relationship
and ready for a different journey.

There is blessing to be discovered
when the words which leave us,
even in our brokenness,
are rooted in love and generosity,
and knit together to bind and fasten.
And we may find
an unexpected harvest to reap,
grounded in grace.

Morning Prayer

Treat others as you mean to be treated, You said.
Then You went one step further
and commanded us to love one another.
In the day ahead, whatever it may hold,
may I be mindful of those I meet,
remembering they too are on a journey
and that we are, friend and stranger,
companions on the road of life.
Grant me the grace to deal with them
as You so graciously deal with me.   AMEN

Evening Prayer

Lord God
I turn my back now
on all that has separated me from You
this day;
on my unkindness and selfishness,
on my choosing to go back
rather than forward with You,
on the times I went my own way,
and ignored Your calling.
In Your grace I turn to You now.
Bind me to You this night
that I may be assured of Your presence
wherever life may lead me.   AMEN

Scripture Readings

Ruth 1:8   *As you have dealt with me*
John 14:27   *Peace I leave with you*

Blessing

May the God of grace
go with us
along the road of life.
May the God of goodness
deal kindly with us
as we seek to be a blessing to others,
and may we meet our Creator
at every turn.   AMEN

Praying in pain

[Hannah] was deeply distressed and prayed to the
Lord, and wept bitterly.

~ 1 Samuel 1:10 ~

Meditation

It went on, year after year.
This bullying, this persistent
provocative name-calling-torture:
sharp words belittling that
precious part of me,
so cherished and revered,
now full-empty with perceived failure.

I was alone.

Even small acts of kindness
couldn't console such deep despair.
The caress of a hand
served to strengthen my isolation.
I would always be an outsider
in my community, rejected
from the womb of my family.

No patient petitions for me, then.

I am spent with sobbing.
Weak with weeping I
hurl my hurt,
roar my rage,
my deep sadness,
pure, livid, strong, unbullied,
straight from my heart to Yours,
dear God.

Morning Prayer

In moments of isolation and loneliness today,
I pray for inner strength, deep solace.
With all who are bullied, or harassed,
who feel belittled or lessened,
I pray for solace-strength deep within.

Bring to birth in each moment of this day,
loving God, the power and resilience
of love conceived deep within.   AMEN

Evening Prayer

Dear God,
I give thanks for all that You have brought to birth
in our world today:
for unexpected moments of joy and delight,
for that sense of deep community
that banishes loneliness and welcomes the outsider.

And I give thanks for each child born in our world –
may they find a place to belong,
and a calling to be leaders,
with Hannah and Samuel,
and all who go before us,
in Your kingdom of peace and justice.   AMEN

Scripture Readings

1 Samuel 1:1–18   *Praying in pain*
Matthew 19:27–30   *Leaving things behind*

Blessing

God of all,
of the insider, of the outsider,
shower Your blessings on any
who are rejected, bullied,
or left outside the community of belonging,
this day and always.   AMEN

Healing touch

*She said to herself, 'If I only touch His cloak, I will be
made well.'*

~ Matthew 9:21 ~

Meditation

Dead weight,
drained of life's blood,
desperate,
desiring death at times and the promise it brings,
jailed in flesh, a cruel confinement:
the heat, the smell,
the humiliation.

He had taken water from a Samaritan woman,
a common cup;
He had raised a woman bent over,
giving new life;
He had healed the daughter of a Syrian woman,
honouring a woman's faith;
why not me?

Unconcerned that my impurity will soil Him
(it's too late for that);
unconcerned – seeing me –
to me He said, 'Take heart'.
Touched by tender transcendence,
seeing, feeling,
alive to the Sacred within me;
in my suffering, imprisonment,
I am loved, embraced, cherished.

Morning Prayer

Rise Sun,
banish my darkness,
gaze once more into my face,
replenish my memory of acceptance,
Your warmth in the heat of the day,
Your soul with mine.
May I perceive moments of miracle
and inner renewal.   AMEN

Evening Prayer

Bless those burdened this night,
women, children and men,
isolated and alone,
craving *shalom*, Sacred peace.
May sleep (my sleep)
be restorative:
like the love of a friend,
the caress of a lover,
the contentment that comes from
Wisdom's hushed whisper.   AMEN

Scripture Readings

Matthew 9:18–22   *Healing touch*
Luke 13:10–17   *A Sabbath healing*

Blessing

Triune God,
Artist, Poet and Lover,
lift me each day
from all that diminishes;
grant me strength,
to paint my story with love
and, with compassion,
dare to dream and live a better world.   AMEN

The edge of life

The demons begged.

~ Matthew 8:31 ~

Meditation

People drift in and out of my life.
They use me and abuse me.
'Maybe I'm just an attention seeker…' my post reads.
Embarrassment and shame
push me closer and closer to the edge.

So-called friends scroll past,
as the demons beg.
I'm still waiting for someone to deliver me.
'Get a life,' the chat snaps,
if only that were it – I could live with that.

The life I live, you couldn't possibly imagine.
So many voices,
clamouring for my attention,
a cacophony of derision I cannot ignore,
telling me this life is not for living,
reminding me of my unworthiness.
Swiping me left and right,
pushing me further towards the edge.

The edge of life is where I live
– if you can call it living –
alone with my begging demons,
wondering whether they
will finally consume me.

Morning Prayer

When life threatens to engulf us
and we cry to You for mercy, God,
You answer us.
We don't always have the ability
to see You where we are,
but let us give thanks
knowing that You are there with us
no matter what.
Bless to us this day,
whatever may unravel.   AMEN

Evening Prayer

Tonight, we remember those who will struggle to sleep.
For those whose minds cannot rest;
for those whose anxiety takes over;
for those who circle the floor
stumbling in the darkness of confusion;
for those who feel that there is no rest
while their very being cries out
for mercy and peace;
may You be there, God,
tonight, and every night.   AMEN

Scripture Readings

Matthew 8:31   *Pleading to be cast out*
Psalm 139:8   *God is with us in the peaks and valleys
of life*

Blessing

May the God of the edges meet you where you are.
May the God of peace bless your inner strife.
May the God of love be balm to your wounds.
May the God of life meet you on the edge.
Loving you, whoever you are.   AMEN

Joy in my heart

'My soul magnifies the Lord,
and my spirit rejoices in God my Saviour.'

~ Luke 1:46–47 ~

Meditation

The outsider, deeply touched by God;
the breaker of marriage convention,
given wisdom and joy beyond measure.
As I think of Mary, I ponder:
what makes my spirit rejoice within me?
What brings me that lightness of being and depth of joy?
That feeling that all is well,
that life can be good and unfold just as intended;
that I have a place;
that my life has meaning and purpose,
delight and depth.
Joy of joys!

Let me rejoice,
That my heart may echo the heart of Mary;
that I may carry the Christ-light within me
and birth love, unconditional and accepting;
experience joy, through the labour of humility;
and know the blessing of God.

Morning Prayer

Loving God,
thank You for another morning,
another chance to live life as well as I can manage;
another day
feeling that I am part of a magnificent song
that began so long before me.

May I glorify You,
discovering You ahead and around me
in the encounters of the day;
meeting me in unexpected ways,
lighting both my own path and that of others.

Bless me, O Living One,
that I may take this praise into my day,
finding meaning, direction and purpose
as I embody Your love.   AMEN

Evening prayer

O generous, caring God,
where did I find You today?
When did Your light shine for me?
How was my soul nourished and delighted?

May my spirit be nurtured
in this time, in this space dedicated to You.
Restore my soul in the depth of sleep,
that I may rise to delight in You in my living.   AMEN

Scripture Readings

Luke 1:46–55   *Mary's song of joy*
Philippians 4:4–8   *Gentleness and joy*

Blessing

May God's blessing rest upon you.
May God's peace abide within you.
May God's presence illuminate your heart.
May your soul magnify the Lord.   AMEN

Together we pray with

PEOPLE IN POWER

*All the kings of the earth shall praise You, O Lord,
for they have heard the words of Your mouth.*

~ Psalm 138:4 ~

Prayer of dedication

*So that all the peoples of the earth may know Your name
and fear You ... and so that they may know that Your name
has been invoked on this house that I have built.*

~ 1 Kings 8:43 ~

Meditation

Within these walls
centuries of stories are roomed:

great tales
of national pride,
of kings, queens, warriors, and heroes
who allowed their lives
to become entwined with the communities they represented,
and each word and action
offering collective voice
to bring peace and contentment to the time
in which they walked;

the community myths
of rites of passage
as birth, marriage and death
journey with
hope, joy and grief,
excitement, love and pain,
and find a resting place
within the qualities of each generation;

the hidden sagas
of those who have sought support
for individual causes
or relief from their anxieties.

Within these walls
each narrative is embraced
and incorporated within the greater epic
of the history of faith,

as minor details offer moments of wonder and awe,
as the Creator's part is revealed.

Morning Prayer

God of tent and temple,
You are not contained within the holy spaces
human hands have made.
Instead You walk within and around us,
shaping the tasks of each day.
Keep us from controlling Your inspiration
so that we become all that You invite us to be.   AMEN

Evening Prayer

Today, within this flesh,
You spurred me to new heights
and comforted me in the depths.
In the changing light and texture of this evening,
may Your Spirit draw my eyes
to catch a glimpse of where You call attention
to the world,
so that this skin may be rebuilt
with new verve for tomorrow's tasks.   AMEN

Scripture Readings

1 Kings 8:23–53   *Dedicating Solomon's Temple*
Revelation 21:1–7   *A new heaven and a new earth*

Blessing

Bless the housing of human skin
that wonders at creation's frame
and looks in awe at the greatness of God's temple.
AMEN

Power of prayer

But Moses' hands grew weary; so they took a stone and put it under him, and he sat on it. Aaron and Hur held up his hands, one on one side, and the other on the other side; so his hands were steady until the sun set.

~ Exodus 17:12 ~

Meditation

An odd battle this,
won by the teamwork of Moses, Aaron, Hur and Joshua.
All over the world, people fight
for survival, for justice, for better conditions;
others fight ruthlessly for power, influence, property.
People fight against poverty and persecution;
others fight foolishly against change and chimeras.

In prayer, we join God's army of saint and angel and
ordinary folk who do this kingdom work.
Doing it together, we hold up one another's hands
in praise and prayer.
As children, we are given simple rules for prayer.
As we age, things become less tidy –
we discover different ways of praying,
trying to discern God's strategy
in our lives and in the lives of others.
We come to value the support of other people,
in our congregations, in smaller groups,
perhaps the mutual support of one other person.
This can be hard work, as Aaron and Hur discovered.

Prayer can be a delight, if always a discipline;
but the hardest work has already been done by our Lord Jesus,
who still prays with us and for us in heaven

Morning Prayer

Lord God, You know the tasks that lie before me today.
You know the work that challenges a nation and its leaders.

We pray for all in high positions, that they may follow wise
and honest strategies, and find the support they deserve.
Guide our MPs, our MSPs, our councillors and public servants.
Bless those who, like Aaron and Hur, support them on either side.
May those who raise their voices on social media
also raise their hands in prayer.

And may I, like Your servant Moses,
have the wisdom to know good from evil,
to be patient with the faults and follies of others,
but faithful in the fight for justice. Amen

Evening Prayer

I hold up my hands, confess my shortcomings ...
I hold up my hands, praise Your patience,
Your welcome, Your forgiveness ...
I hold up my hands, remember those in need
and in the thick of things ...

O God our Father, and the Father of our Lord Jesus,
show me what was true this day and what was not;
show me who was faithful, who was false;
show me where the battles lay
in which my head and heart and hand should have been.
Make known Your name,
even the name of Jesus in which together we pray. Amen

Scripture Readings

Exodus 17:8–16 *The power of prayer*
John 17:1–24 *The intimacy of prayer*

Blessing

May God grant you wisdom
in what you lift and what you lay down.
May God grant you strength
to do this kindly and fruitfully.
And may God grant you the grace of companionship
in all that you do. Amen

Let them fall!

*'Lord God, remember me and strengthen me only
this once, O God, so that with this one act of revenge
I may pay back the Philistines for my two eyes.'*

~ Judges 16:28 ~

Meditation

Battered and beaten as I've been
the plaything of heartless heretics,
Godless gloaters, proud and untouchable,
emptying me of dignity,
sucking out all joy,
perversely delighted in my shrinking.

Violated, I need vindication.
Abused, I need an advocate.
Alone, I need an ally.

In my degradation there is no justice.
In their exaltation there is no goodness.
My broken heart must not be snuffed out
but sing its God-honest song:
'Let them fall!'

Morning Prayer

I rise as the shell of what I once was.
Do You see what they've done to me, God?
See the ruin, the brokenness, the limping they've caused!
These enemies of Yours, these enemies of mine.

Why pretend that I'm mercifully minded?
You see my heart as clearly as You see their crimes.
So I'll give voice to what's there –
no more bubbling up in a hidden cauldron.
I'll just say it, God, honest and impure:
'Let them fall!'

Let my life be in Your hands.
Let their lives be in Your hands.
Let that be enough for me.
Let me trust that Your wisdom, power, sovereignty and mercy
are greater than my feelings.
Give me strength today, one more time,
to do what I could not do without You.   AMEN

Evening Prayer

Where else can I go but to You, O Lord?
Who else will listen to me if You will not?
Yet my heart hopes in this:
You hear my cry, and You are my salvation.
Let me rest in that.

You are stronger than every foe.
You'll set all things right as Your kingdom comes.
Let me rest in that.

I have poured out to You the pain and the offence
in real, red-blooded prayer.
I have such little power and such little mercy;
You have infinite stores of both.
Let me rest in that.   AMEN

Scripture Readings

Judges 16:23–30   *Let them fall!*
Psalm 59   *Deliver me from them*

Blessing

May the Lord be to us
our strength, our shield, our fortress;
our rescuer, our healer, our comforter;
our witness, our advocate, our judge;
our daily bread and our eternal hope.   AMEN

Self-righteous boasting

'God, I thank You that I am not like other people ...'
~ Luke 18:11 ~

Meditation

There he is, the Pharisee,
loudly dictating a prayer
to the virtual assistant on his phone,
'Sarai – open my prayer app!'
He would be the guy in the train carriage
with one of those things clipped to his ear,
talking into a device that is
perched precariously on pinstripe
– threatening to shatter.
In the middle of the 'quiet coach'.
Everyone forced to listen to his boasting.
'Thank You for making me an achiever!' he would bark,
the phone stuttering and lagging
as it struggles to catch up.
'Thank You for making me a team player
and a natural leader and a go-getter
with a drive to succeed! Thank God!
Thank You for giving me no sense of humour
or self-awareness, or irony, or perspective.
I pray for others – that I don't
intimidate them with my giftedness.
I pray for others – that they are not too
disheartened – not to be me.'

Where does this guy get off? They'd be thinking.
Hopefully the next stop ...
But the Pharisee is unfazed, clueless.
Spectacularly, exquisitely wrong.
He's at least grateful, which means
he may be some of the way there –
even if he's facing the wrong direction ...

Morning Prayer

Be with us this morning
through our arrogance
and immodesty
and vanity.
Help us to laugh at ourselves,
keeping our enthusiasm
while refining it.   Amen

Evening Prayer

Loving, gracious God,
thank You for bearing with us today
even when we have been embarrassing and awkward,
or have made a fool of ourselves.
Harness our enthusiasms tomorrow
and give us a dose of reality
when we need it.   Amen

Scripture Readings

Luke 18:11–12   *Self-righteous boasting*
Proverbs 27:1–2   *Let another praise You*

Blessing

Bless our boundless (and
often misplaced) enthusiasm
and direct it to Your purposes
in Your loving wisdom.   Amen

'It' – prayer for a dying son

... and it became very ill.

~ 2 Samuel 12:15 ~

Meditation

It was the 6th of September 1951.
Thursday's child is supposed to have far to go.
But my baby son's life was cruelly short,
a measure of mere minutes.
I never got to see his face – he was bundled away
like a pound of yesterday's mince.
No chance to say goodbye – just an expectation
that I'd get on with it
that it was for the best
and I could have another.
But, there is no other – like your first born.
I still plead with God
as I did the day he was born.
I would have traded power, wealth, anything –
for life itself.
The wounds of his birth and death are still
so painfully raw...

But the thing I will never forget, for as long as I live,
the careless language
that denied his existence – when the nurse called him 'it'
as if the life in him had never existed.

Morning Prayer

It's often said, God,
that parents would do anything for their child.
Anything.
Sometimes, there is nothing that can be done.
You know that pain of loss in the death of Your Son.
Cradle in Your arms those who struggle with pain and loss.
Speak tenderly to them when our human words fail.
May Your grace, love and comfort encircle them,
every day.   AMEN

Evening Prayer

We all have moments when we would bargain with God.
Times when we will happily trade all that we have
and all that we are, just for one more gasp of life.
In our times of despair and loss,
as the darkness threatens to engulf us,
bring to us the dawn of a new day –
a sign that You are present in our heartbreak.   AMEN

Scripture Readings

2 Samuel 12:15-17   *David pleads with God for his son*
Revelation 21:4   *The ultimate comfort in Christ's coming*

Blessing

May God cradle you in love.
May God gently comfort you.
May God whisper tenderly to you.
And may God bring you peace.   AMEN

Job – a soul's aching

'I would choose strangling and death rather than this body. I loathe my life.'

~ Job 7:15–16 ~

Meditation

Groaning,
a soul's aching:
nothing in life has been worth this price.
Is there a greater torment
than to watch disease
corrupt my beloved, my life?
I hate death's potion.
I hate this world's brutality,
savagery, senselessness.
God is Love?
I want to hit God,
hit God,
as, in rage, a boxer assaults a punch bag.

Give me the deadness of the graveyard.
I envy the lifeless,
mown down, unable to suffer loss any more,
protected now from the pretence that life will be good.
I live in darkness unrelieved.

It is dishonest, facile,
to deny Job his voice,
to reduce resurrection to cliché.
There is a time to listen for Eternity's whisper,
for the God whose wisdom is greater than mine.
That Silence will come
but only after I can be true to myself;
not until I am exhausted with no more punches
to throw.

Morning Prayer

Holy God,
Mystery buried deeper than all that mind can fathom,
more sublime, primaeval
than doctrine's tight confines;
through story, mask and veil,
reveal me to myself
maturing beyond obsession, anxiety,
envy, resentment and fear;
every step a prayer,
every vista a meditation,
every breath the Breath of God.   AMEN

Evening Prayer

Eternal Lover,
grant me emptiness that reveals myself to me,
that I may escape voices haunting the mind,
mocking, threatening, disturbing.
In syllables known only to the heart
let me hear Eternity's silence and,
like Job,
discover the Presence
hidden in view,
elusive, imperceptible and intimate;
my soul's resurrection.   AMEN

Scripture Readings

Job 7:7–21   *Job's torment*
Mark 15:25–37   *Cry of dereliction*

Blessing

May we draw strength from Job's lament;
be shaped by his honesty,
confidence and integrity;
and never forget that, in the end,
God felt his pain, heard his scream and
restored his soul.   AMEN

Wrestling with God

Do what is just ...

~ Genesis 18:25 ~

Meditation

Should we wrestle with God?
How do we comprehend movement
in the mind of the Almighty?
If the peace of God passes all understanding,
how may we, in faith, in conscience,
hope to grasp God's power to act
with justice and with mercy?

Our judgement is often arbitrary and based
on prejudice and shallow understanding.
We claim a world of black and white,
when all around is grey and hazed.
God, at last, hears Abraham's call for mercy
when Abraham shares concern for the souls of Sodom,
where innocent and guilty are enmeshed
so closely.

Is God's judgement on the people to be based on
the guilt of the many, or the innocence of the few?
And in our world today, when we pass judgement,
what tempers our response?
Do we strain our mercy and debase its quality,
or do we do what is just, love kindness,
and walk humbly with our God?

Morning Prayer

Judge and Mercy-giver,
today we will pass judgement upon
our fellow human beings:
the people who let us down;
the people who cause hurt;
the people who break lives and hope.

As we stand to accuse, and sometimes with good cause,
let us search out the possibility of redemption,
that in each lost soul
there may yet be some unseen cause
that may explain, if not excuse the action.
And if we judge,
make us aware of what we say and think and do,
and wonder who, in this stark world,
might find a place for hope and new beginning.
Lord have mercy,
Christ have mercy,
Lord have mercy.   AMEN

Evening Prayer

Eternal God,
into Your hands we place the wholeness
and the brokenness of this day.
We pray for justice to roll down like rivers,
and mercy like an overflowing stream
to purge and cleanse and make things new
that have been soiled or maimed or tarnished.
Renewing God, refresh, restore, remake,
and settle in our hearts the thirst for justice,
to make our world, our lives, the home of fairness.
In Jesus' powerful Name.   AMEN

Scripture Readings

Genesis 18:23–32   *Wrestling with God*
Matthew 15:21–28   *Crumbs of hope*

Blessing

Come Holy God,
fill our lives
with peace, hope and joy;
today, tonight, and forever.   AMEN

Knowing God

*Moses said to the Lord ... 'Show me Your ways, so that
I may know You and find favour in Your sight.'*

~ Exodus 33:12–13 ~

Meditation

Stepping
outside the camp,
away from interruptions and distractions,
concerns and loves immediate and everyday,
Moses, servant of God, lawgiver and legend,
entered the Tent of the Presence.
Encountering Eternity,
the paradox of nothing and No-thing,
intimate with the Sacred.
At one, soul to Soul
in the pillar-like cloud,
eclipsing Eternity;
darkness to Darkness,
silence to Silence,
in the myth the mystery of
the *Shekinah*, indwelling Presence,
hovering.

On the mountain top,
in the tent,
present Yourself;
be present
in the long grasses jostling,
the Dance of the Trinity;
in Holy Writ, in suggestions,
and hints,
and margins for imagination,
the sublime strokes of the Artist.

Morning Prayer

Go with me this day
that I may perceive You
in my own moments of miracle:
in the bush burning ahead of me,
in the walls of water on my journey,
in the darkness of my being,
the darkness of my faith and
the darkness of the Divine.
Open my heart to Your labyrinthine subtlety:
the Invisible emerging imperceptibly.   AMEN

Evening Prayer

In rest and relaxation,
in the unconscious realm of dreams,
comfort and hold me,
heal and restore me,
that, blessed by *shalom*, a shower of peace,
I may leave the Tent of Presence,
rise refreshed,
an aura of light, Divine essence,
shining within me.   AMEN

Scripture Readings

Exodus 33:12–13, 15–16   *Knowing God*
Genesis 28:10–17   *Jacob at Bethel*

Blessing

Like Moses,
may I glimpse the Holy One.
Mystery beyond mysteries,
Wisdom words cannot capture.
Lover beyond compare,
show me Your ways:
deepen my understanding;
embrace me with Eternity's silence.   AMEN

Together we pray with

THE PSALMISTS

To You, O Lord, I lift up my soul.

~ Psalm 25:1 ~

How long?

Will You forget me forever?

~ Psalm 13:1–2 ~

Meditation

Where have You gone?

Hello?

Is anyone there?

Show up, will You?

Because I can't hold out.
Because I am going under.
Because nothing is easing
this pain, pain, pain.
Because I thought You cared.
Because I am seeking and I do not find.
Because I am asking and I am not given.
Because I am knocking and the door stays shut.
Because I'm scared.
Your absence sends me into sickening freefall.
Your silence is a black hole of dread.
Don't I matter to You?
Don't You see me anymore?
Have I dropped off Your radar?

Hello?

Morning Prayer

How dare You?
After all Your promises?
Your presence is forever?
You'll always be here?
You never sleep?
So what's this?

Absent,
silent,
dormant God.

I'm not asking for earthquake, wind or fire,
but give me a whisper, a clue, a crumb.
Soon?   AMEN

Evening Prayer

God,
again I'm here,
and again You're not.

Why do I still talk into this nothingness?
Why don't I conclude there is no God?
I've survived another day without You.
Why don't I give up?

But I know You.
Though sometimes I wish I didn't.
In spite of everything,
this emptiness cannot last.
Don't stay hidden.
Don't keep me waiting forever.
You promised, remember?   AMEN

Scripture Readings

> Psalm 13   *Protesting God's absence*
> Job 30:20–31   *When God does nothing to help*

Blessing

> God, bless us while You're gone,
> because even Your absence
> is better than
> nothing.   AMEN

Listen to my cry

Give ear to my words, O Lord; give heed to my sighing.
Listen to the sound of my cry, my King and my God,
   for to You I pray.

~ Psalm 5:1–2 ~

Meditation

God's people discover a new morning
scattered across the grey paths of the world;
trying to hang on to its beauty as it becomes
jagged at the edges;
ending up grieved at the things that are making each day
so hard for so many people,
grieved at their own inability to make much of a difference.

Such grief is part of what we take to God in prayer.
The Psalms give us a language for regret,
a language for frustration, a language for our complaints.
Left in our hearts, grief may fester,
compassion may dry up;
taken to God, grief finds safe lodging,
and compassion fresh fuel.

The new day – a time for us to salute our God
in the cosmic temple created
for God's delight and our enjoyment.
The new day – a time to praise our God
in the slender temple of our hearts.
The new day – a time to share our feelings
with the God of heaven and earth.

Morning Prayer

Today O Lord:
help me to find the simplicity of Your call
in the midst of preoccupation.
Help me to see the wonder of Your provision
in the details of the day.

Help me to share the delight You take in everything good.
As I expect You to hear my tiny voice,
so may I listen to the people few will notice,
and discover the presence of Jesus. AMEN

Evening Prayer

Where my path has been straight,
I acknowledge Your good purpose for me.
Where my path has been up and down,
I thank You for Your strength.
Where my path has been crooked,
I seek Your mercy and guidance.

Your word, O God,
so wonderfully embraces those who seek You,
blesses the hungry, sad and poor in spirit,
tests the hearts of all.
Your word is thrown like seed throughout the world,
on soils and situations of all kinds.
Your word is seed and fuel, plea and provision,
a cone waiting for the fire in which it will germinate.
Tonight I am with the world's poor,
hungry for Your word of mercy, help and blessing.
I am excited ... I am sobered ... but also comforted. AMEN

Scripture Readings

Psalm 5:1–8   *Hear me, lead me*
Matthew 5:1–11   *The truly blessed*

Blessing

God grant us the curiosity of a child,
the courage of a deep sea diver,
the compassion of Jesus,
the conviction that all shall be well
and all things work out for good. AMEN

Making space

O Lord, who may abide in Your tent?

~ Psalm 15:1 ~

Meditation

When I need to make space,
downsize and declutter –
it's so much easier said than done.
Is that not what attics are for?
So much easier to hold onto things
than let go …

But if I make space,
I have room –
room for something else.

You make space for me, God.
You welcome me in –
no questions asked.
You rejoice to offer me a home
in You.

So how will I fill my space?
With just another distraction,
or some replacement clutter?
Can I find room for You?

Morning Prayer

You extend, O God,
a warm and welcoming embrace.
Generation after generation
have found their home in You.
You invite me in,
again and again.

Let Your invitation inspire me,
to offer a welcome to those I meet.

Who is like You?
How can I make You known?

You are found in love
shown for God and one another.
This is Your commandment;
write it on my heart today.   AMEN

Evening Prayer

Secure in the blanket of God,
I offer my prayers this night:
for what I celebrate,
for what I regret,
for those I care for,
for those You call me to care for.
Let my prayers find their home in You.

Secure in the peace of God,
I give thanks for all I have received this day:
a friendly encounter,
a helpful conversation,
a surprising moment,
a sense of Your presence with me.
Let my praise be heard,
for it is offered in love.   AMEN

Scripture Readings

> Psalm 15   *Making space*
> Luke 15:20–24   *Welcome home*

Blessing

> Happy are those who find their home in God.
> May the blessing of sharing space
> with God and with others,
> fill your day with surprise and joy.   AMEN

The strength and peace of the Lord

May the Lord give strength to His people!
May the Lord bless His people with peace!

~ Psalm 29:11 ~

Meditation

Without strength, peace is precarious,
and without peace, strength is callous.

Strength from God, who wrestles with the roots of evil.
Strength from God, who whispers into the troubled heart.
Peace from God, who calls out with grace and wisdom.
Peace from God, who sets the ground rules of fellowship.

Without strength, peace is precarious,
and without peace, strength is callous.

Strength to those who struggle with the growth of oppression.
Strength to those who comfort those with a weight of anxiety.
Peace to those who broker deals with kingdom rules.
Peace to those who speak what is right to those in power.

Without strength, peace is precarious,
and without peace, strength is callous.

Strength to those who lift up the world before God.
Strength to those who pray in hope of freedom.
Peace to those who seek God's grace and wisdom.
Peace to those who yearn for companionship.

Morning Prayer

God, I would interpret 'Your people' generously,
and pray for all who carry the burdens of responsibility,
of poverty, of pain, of danger, of persecution.

May they have the strength to survive, to forgive,
to govern, to live in hope against all odds.
May they find peace beyond their understanding,
a peace that empowers them and amazes others,
through Jesus Christ our living, loving Lord.   AMEN

Evening Prayer

Day and night You are praised
in ways beyond our present seeing,
God of past, God of now, God of time to come.
Let me be part of that heavenly swirl of thanksgiving.
Let me be part of that heavenly waterfall of praise.
And while I sleep, let me breathe in Your strength,
breathe out Your peace, my heart and lungs
full of the wind of Your Spirit.   AMEN

Scripture Readings

> Psalm 29:1–11   *God speaks to creation*
> Revelation 4:1–11   *Creation speaks to God*

Blessing

> God almighty,
> who was and is and is to come:
> make clear our past,
> make quiet our now,
> make sure our morrow.
> And to our Lord and God
> be glory and honour for ever.   AMEN

Praising God even though ...

Yet You have broken us in the haunt of jackals ...

~ Psalm 44:19 ~

Meditation

I met You
under the cover of darkness.
I first beheld You in the haunt of jackals
among thorny ground,
a place of howls
and lacerating cold.
The still night all around,
a carapace of loneliness
with only brother jackal for company.

I meet You here once more,
with
frostbitten lips
mouthing
frostbitten
worship.
I don't know if You are sleeping
but I am wide awake
watching for the morning,
with only brother jackal as witness.

I am broken
open
with praise
that will not cease
in this place of darkness.
After all it was in this place
I first beheld You
and I know
You will honour
our old meeting place.

Morning Prayer

Holy One of all places and all times,
accompany us in desolation and depression and despair
as You are with us in joy and celebration and love.
Meet us in the old familiar parts of our soul,
well trodden and well worn,
where we cry out for Your guidance. AMEN

Evening Prayer

Be with us as we go into this night,
praising You
despite our painful memories
and careworn fears,
alone amongst our lonelinesses.
Come alongside us,
we pray. AMEN

Scripture Readings

> Psalm 44   *Praising God even though ...*
> Job 30:16–31   *I cry and You do not answer*

Blessing

> We call upon You for Your blessing
> even when all feels remote and strange
> – unknown and unknowable –
> we call upon Your blessing
> with broken open hearts.   AMEN

Asaph – songs for justice

Rescue the weak and the needy;
deliver them from the hand of the wicked.

~ Psalm 82:4 ~

Meditation

Asaph, musician-psalmist,
created laments,
voicing the struggles of his people;
helping them sing of their distress and despair;
allowing their emotions to flow;
reconnecting them with God's past faithfulness,
so that hope might emerge from their hearts.

Psalms, the prayer book of Jesus,
where He heard of the times when His ancestors were
poor in spirit, worn out, at the end of their tether,
weak and needy, deeply afraid, even tormented.
Jesus knew from the very core of His own experience
that God loves us when we are low and poor.

Psalms teach us the passionate language of prayer:
that anger is natural and normal;
that cries for justice are transformed in the crucible of prayer,
bringing life – within us and through us;
that God is present, ever present,
hearing, listening, even when it seems otherwise;
that God never leaves or forsakes the needy and weak;
that God is present,
ever present.

Morning Prayer

Hear me, O God,
hear my songs of lament
at injustices
too many, too overwhelming,
crowding in on me.

How can there be so much pain and violence?
Will it ever end?
Will we never learn?
Receive the emotions that churn around in me
when I open myself to such questions.
Listen to my heartfelt pleas for peace, for justice.

May I listen today with all of creation
for the joy and life at the heart of all being.
May this rhythm sustain me throughout today.
May Your song carry me;
the praise that underpins all of creation
delight my heart
and allow my voice to join with my ancestors,
my sisters and brothers
and all of creation,
as we seek justice for all.   AMEN

Evening Prayer

God of justice,
You bring order and meaning when the time is right;
God of love,
teach me to rest in You.
Sing me to sleep with a peace beyond all understanding
and a knowledge that You are ever present.   AMEN

Scripture Readings

Psalm 82:2–4   *Plea for justice*
Lamentations 5   *Restore us to Yourself*

Blessing

May Your justice resound,
Your grace and mercy sing aloud,
Your peace be spoken
over all who need to know
Your love and presence.   AMEN

Music to my ears!

Let everything that breathes praise the Lord!

~ Psalm 150:6 ~

Meditation

In every murmur,
every gentle whisper,
every beating pulse,
every pounding heartbeat,
is the melody of creation
in all its glory.

In every planet,
every creature,
every flicker of existence,
every hint of being,
is the symphony of the Creator
in all generosity and greatness.

I am but one note
in this magnum opus of life,
yet join with joy nature's song,
that it may reverberate with praise.

Morning Prayer

As I take the first breaths of the day, Lord,
without thought or attention,
may I pause for a moment and remember
as I inhale and exhale,
as my lungs fill with fresh air,
as my heart beats within my chest
and as my body and brain
engage with the wonder of creation,
that You are the source of all life.
May I draw You in and breathe You out
in all I do today and every day
so that my praise may be music to Your ears.   AMEN

Evening Prayer

I am a small part of Your creation, Lord,
yet carefully scripted
and gifted my own refrain
with which to play.
If I have wasted one breath today
on careless talk,
if my life has been discordant
through my action or inaction,
then forgive me.
Speak Your soothing rhythm
deep into my soul this night
that tomorrow I may reprise my part
in harmony with Your purpose.   AMEN

Scripture Readings

Psalm 150   *Music to my ears!*
Ephesians 5:19–20   *Making melody to God*

Blessing

From the heights to the depths,
from the silence to the noise,
from the first to the final breath,
may we know blessing and grace,
through our Lord Jesus Christ.   AMEN

Together we pray with

WORSHIPPERS

'God is spirit, and those who worship Him must worship in spirit and truth'

~ John 4:24 ~

Elizabeth blesses Mary

*'And blessed is she who believed that there would be a
fulfilment of what was spoken to her by the Lord.'*

~ Luke 1:45 ~

Meditation

Last night in prayer,
with head bowed,
eyes closed,
and hands loosely held,
I prayed with all my heart to be able to accept
the news of today.
There were no expectations on my lips,
but a plea
to live with the day that came.

The morning light has awoken,
and Your goodness and promise have astonished me.
The doubts and uncertainty of longing for more
have been relieved;
for accepting this gift of life You offer
does not mean limitation.
Instead, the potential sparks and delights,
bursting with energy
for what is still to come.

Morning Prayer

In the morning light,
Creator God,
the earth seems fresh and full of possibility.
May the energies of this moment
be used wisely,
and take all of the wonder found in You
to ask questions of the world.

Let my voice speak
of the hope and promise
that should bring light and life
to all.   AMEN

Evening Prayer

The darkness seems almost womblike,
Tender Maker.
Snuggling in to find the place of comfort,
the rush and pump of blood around
do not bring an easy mind.
The fresh thoughts of the morning
have been shared, and grown, and stirred,
and in fading light the excitement has diminished.
May this rest not be selfish,
but instead make room
for another day
where Your words are spoken in love.   AMEN

Scripture Readings

Luke 1:39–45   *Mary's visit to Elizabeth*
Acts 9:15–19   *Ananias' visit to Paul*

Blessing

May we be blessed by the life of God
found in the gift of other people,
as the gospel is given voice
and the Spirit's joy is sung.   AMEN

'Yes, Lord, I believe'

[Martha] said to Him, 'Yes, Lord, I believe that You are the Messiah, the Son of God, the one coming into the world.'

~ John 11:27 ~

Meditation

'Do you believe this?' He asked.
Was He asking me to trust
that what was lost would return?
That my brother who was dead would live again?
How could I possibly believe such a fantasy?
      And yet something in the way He spoke
      compelled me to say yes.

'Do you believe this?'
What would have happened if I had said no?
How badly would
my confidence have been knocked,
my faith dealt a blow?
      It was something in the power of His presence
      that meant I said 'Yes, Lord.'

'Do you believe this?' He asked.
Every cell in my body, each hair on my head,
each tear and wail of grief was pleading –
'Yes – oh yes, please let this be true. And let my brother live.'

When I allowed myself to believe
that He was the Messiah;
that He spoke with
an authority and a confidence that offered
neither the promise of an easy passage,
nor a predictable future,
but a faith-journey unfurling,
then I knew that I could
confess with conviction: 'Yes, I believe.'

Morning Prayer

This morning I confess my unbelief:
the times when I have questioned without listening,
or scorned without compassion –
and ask Your forgiveness,
dear Lord.

This morning I confess my doubts:
as I move into the fullness of the day,
may I travel with the strength of a faith
that embraces doubt and
welcomes questions,
enfolding them in a love that accepts all.   AMEN

Evening Prayer

May I move towards the night
grateful for all that has been;
hopeful for all that is yet to come;
faithful to the end of my days.

May I move towards the night
resting in the power of Jesus' love;
confessing with Martha and all
His followers: 'Yes, Lord, I believe.'   AMEN

Scripture Readings

John 11:21–27   *'Yes, Lord, I believe'*
1 Timothy 6:11–16   *Keep the faith*

Blessing

May the blessing of our Lord Jesus Christ,
in whose presence we take hope,
in whose life we find inspiration,
be with us and remain with us
now and always.   AMEN

Time after terrible time

'Lord, do not hold this sin against them!'

~ Acts 7:60 ~

Meditation

Stones.
Knives.
Guns.
Bombs.

Acid.
Arson.
White van.
Poison.

Unprovoked attack.
Mob violence.
Premeditated murder.
War.

Persecution.
Prejudice.
Racial hatred.
Genocide.

Despite our best efforts.
Life support.
No remains found.
Died instantly.

Do not.
Do not hold.
Do not hold this sin.
Do not hold this sin against them.

Morning Prayer

Dear God,
what worse way do people betray You
than by killing each other.
Life is sacred, but murder is never out of the news.
Still, please keep our hearts open
and soft,
time after terrible time;
may we be well practised in answering brutality
with peace
and again peace,
that we may live up to being Your children.   AMEN

Evening Prayer

Gracious God,
be with the ones who today
turned their backs on revenge,
did not take a life for a life,
refused to escalate violence,
did not permit hatred to take hold.
Be with the ones who tonight
sit with Your impossible ask of forgiving.
Deep as they are wounded,
pour Your love deeper still.   AMEN

Scripture Readings

Acts 7:51–60   *Stephen's dying prayer*
Luke 6:27–36   *Tough advice from Jesus*

Blessing

God's blessing on those who curse,
persecute, hate or kill.
God's blessing on each one.   AMEN

A costly offering

The house was filled with the fragrance of the perfume.
~ John 12:3 ~

Meditation

I don't always understand my own motivations,
so I can't always expect others to –
human nature questions the unexpected.

Am I suspicious of generosity?
Do I wonder what lies behind
the motivation of others?
Do I expect people to surprise
or disappointment me?

Living with these questions
and more –
I bring what I am,
and what I might become in God.

I bring what needs to be changed,
knowing it might cost me.

What can I give?
A measure, a portion, my all?

Morning Prayer

God, You awaken my senses to Your presence,
with sight and sound,
taste and smell.
You are in all that brings life,
and I praise You this day.

Let my prayer rise like perfume,
offering something of beauty
to the One who gives joy.

Let what I do and what I say
be uplifting to those I meet.
Let Christ be seen through me.

You are worthy of all my worship.
Accept what I pour out before You
in love. AMEN

Evening Prayer

Extravagant God,
in every moment You are doing something new:
bringing life out of death;
offering light in darkness;
gently encouraging me
to seek and to find You.

As I reflect on this day,
have I made time to worship You?
In my words, in my actions,
have I revealed Your love?

Let me find a way
to not count the cost.
For You have given Your all,
and You are my salvation. AMEN

Scripture Readings

John 12:1–8   *A costly offering*
Ruth 1:16–17   *Generous love*

Blessing

God be in all you give,
With heart, soul, mind and strength,
For God has given you all. AMEN

Mother of Thunder

Then the mother of the sons of Zebedee came to Him
with her sons.

~ Matthew 20:20 ~

Meditation

Here she comes now – the Mother of Thunder* –
mum to the rowdy disciples James and John,
struggling in the eye of the storm
but wanting the best for them.
She's asked for a quick word,
'Yes they are a little boisterous,
but I mean that's all the ... potential
isn't it?'

Jesus is quiet, but His eyes are softening,
a smile flickering across His face,
an eyebrow raising as she asks for them to be moved
to the front row, the top of the class, the best seats.
'They could move this whole enterprise from
"good" to "outstanding" with all their potential.'

He is nodding sympathetically,
appreciating as well as anyone the love
of a parent for their child.
He's thinking
that she's rather like her sons,
impetuous, impertinent, impulsive
but also passionate, loving, crackling with vibrancy.

He stands there,
silently offering witness,
to the generous love
of the Mother of Thunder.

*Mark 3:16–17: *'So he appointed the twelve: ... James son of*
Zebedee and John the brother of James (to whom he gave the name
Boanerges, that is, Sons of Thunder)'

Morning Prayer

Mother God,
be with us through this day
even when we push too hard
or when we get the wrong end of the stick
or when our love blinds us.
Upset our preconceptions
and undermine our assumptions.
And thank You for listening to our requests
however selfish or biased they are.
Continually shape us.   AMEN

Evening Prayer

As we settle ourselves for the night,
soothe our racing minds
that are concerned with status, authority and position.
Help us to understand that proximity to You
is proximity to where You are leading us
and not proximity to a throne of our own imagining.
Lead us to a place of humility and peace.   AMEN

Scripture Readings

| Matthew 20:20–28 | *A mother asking a favour* |
| Psalm 34:15–22 | *The eyes of the Lord are on the righteous* |

Blessing

Grant us new understanding
where old understandings
will simply no longer suffice.   AMEN

Bread of heaven

'Sir, give us this bread always.'

~ John 6:34 ~

Meditation

'It sounds good, this bread from heaven –
a way to stop the everyday craving,
a way to fill up the persisting emptiness,
a way to to meet my appetite like nothing on earth ever has.
Let me have it!'

They want the promise.
But do they want the person it is wrapped in?
Bread of Life, Son of God.
Take or leave; eat or pass.

Longing to be gratified,
but not to be justified.
Longing to be satisfied,
but not to be sanctified.

The Bread of Life is more than you asked for,
harder to swallow,
sweeter to taste,
more filling by far,
heavenly satiation,
far surpassing constant earthly grazing.

Morning Prayer

I wake up hungry, Lord Jesus,
hungry for Your presence and the fullness that it brings;
thirsty for Your righteousness reviving parched people.
I come to You this morning for manna,
daily bread to nourish me
for all that You have for me today.

Jesus, as I come to You,
I am filled with peace
about the places I'll go and the people I'll be among;
with confidence about Your presence in each hour;
with hope for the day to play out as You will;
with Your Spirit, enabling me that I might lack nothing.

Fill me up in all the ways You can, Lord Jesus,
that others might taste and see that the Lord is good.   AMEN

Evening Prayer

I go to bed full, Lord Jesus,
full from all that You have provided for me:
material blessings that have sufficed and more;
spiritual blessings when I received what Your hand offered.

In deliberate moments and unexpected ones,
You surprised me afresh
to find how I am fuller
the nearer I am to You.

At the day's eve, let me perceive
more of Your unfathomable love,
that I might be filled to the brim
with the fullness You give;
that tomorrow I might be
all the more discovering and sharing;
that life in Christ is infinitely fuller.   AMEN

Scripture Readings

John 6:25–36   *Jesus fills infinitely*
Ephesians 3:16–19   *The fullness of God's love*

Blessing

May you know Jesus more fully today than ever before.
May you grow in grasping Jesus' love more and more.
May you show an empty world what God has in store.
AMEN

Return to the Lord

*'Stand up and bless the Lord your God from
everlasting to everlasting.'*

~ Nehemiah 9:5 ~

Meditation

Stand up …
Seek the Lord your God!
Praise the Lord your God!
The Creator, the Law-giver, the Liberator.

Teshuvah – 'Return to the Lord.'
The humility of sackcloth and ashes.
A time of repentance;
a time to be honest about our true condition;
of sifting through the baggage and burden of sin.

Teshuvah – 'Return to the Lord.'
A time to make confession;
a time of dying and rising;
of putting right, of being restored.

Teshuvah – 'Return to the Lord.'
A journey that untangles us;
a journey that mends and remedies us.

Stand up…
Return to the Lord your God!
Praise the Lord your God!
The Creator, the Law-giver, the Liberator.

Morning Prayer

Lord God, we bless You for the new day before us.
We stand before You,
wholly present,
even in our fears and failings.
Liberate us to new possibilities.
Refresh us to set our hearts on You.
Stir us with eager spirits to share Your mending of the world.
Lord God, we bless You for the new day before us.   AMEN

Evening Prayer

We return to You
filled with the day.
In the places where we have been hard,
in our show of power and control;
in the places where we have been soft,
in our weakness and frailty;
come and untangle us, free us and mend us.
We pray for solace and forgiveness;
that Your mending will make us whole again.
We return to You,
thankful and overflowing with praise.   AMEN

Scripture Readings

Nehemiah 9:5–38   *Confession and praise*
Hosea 6:1–3   *Return to the Lord*

Blessing

In your returning,
may God open blessings to you;
may God turn to you in love;
may God reach out to you
and raise you up to new life.
Let all the people say:
AMEN

THE SOUND OF PRAYER

TWELVE REFLECTIONS
ON HOW PRAYER IS EXPRESSED
THROUGH SOUND
IN DIFFERENT CIRCUMSTANCES
AND ENVIRONMENTS

There is in souls a sympathy with sounds:
And as the mind is pitch'd the ear is pleased
With melting airs, or martial, brisk or grave;
Some chord in unison with what we hear
Is touch'd within us, and the heart replies.

~ William Cowper, from 'The Winter Walk at Noon' ~

Vibrations

How shall I pray?
Are tears prayers, Lord?
Are screams prayers,
or groans,
or sighs
or curses?

~ Ted Lodder, from 'How Shall I Pray'
in *Guerrillas of Grace* ~

A torrent of noise.

Wave after wave pouring in, battering against all in its path.

The life of a sound wave can be a violent one. Crashing, reverberating, permeating and engulfing. It may even meet itself coming back, pouring scorn upon itself, until stuck in a loop, it screams for escape.

At other times it is a gentler affair. As intimate as a whisper or mezzo piano music dancing gracefully, caressing the ear of the listener until finally settling and resting within.

The listener? Who is that? The one who hears? The one who waits to be told? The truth seeker? The audience? The one with no choice but to bear witness to the noise?

Sometimes we may imagine a kind of blue, or we try to paint it black, but regardless of how much colour we associate with it, we never get to see sound. It is made visible in the reaction of its recipient, bending and bowing to its every whim. The vibrations are felt, whether you are directly in their path or watching others dance in tempo.

As I recall news reports of the Manchester bombing and of the Grenfell Tower disaster flooding our screens, reports of school shootings flashing up on social media feeds and bleeding across broadsheets, I am reluctant to imagine the noise.

It feels indelicate for me to acquaint myself intimately with something that did not affect me directly.

Yet I hear it.I feel it.

Even at great distance, it has not only left its mark, but I recognise its sound. We can be overly familiar with cries of grief, of frustration and hurt, forgetting each has its own voice and character, a melody line of truth and pain that weaves together with other twisting lines to create a dissonant antiphony that is both terrible and inspiring.

The sounds of these recent disasters still echo within the walls of homes, schools and hospitals. They do not lie dormant in cemeteries, mortuaries and ruined buildings. Instead, they ring like tinnitus in the ears of those caught in the first wave. They resonate with those outside the blast radius, who were far from the lick of flame and pillar of smoke, but still recognised the call for help, the need for action and the urgent need for solidarity.

In times of disaster, we invariably hear stories of the generosity and courage of others, whether first responders or communities gathering around those who need support. We hear stories of doors thrown open wide to harbour those needing shelter, of collections of money and supplies. In the midst of this beautiful display of humanity, we hear the blend of new voices, of creative responses, we hear soaring solos, well-rehearsed choirs, we hear improvisation and repetition, sound and fury, and yet still there is the same old rhetoric.

The same empty offering of 'thoughts and prayers'.

And in that space, when something could have been said to temper the litany of denial, political posturing and blaming the other, the opportunity for someone to say something thoughtful and prayerful is missed.

But, the sound of prayer is there.

Beyond the clichéd rumblings of those who need to say something.

It is there.

Perhaps as a whisper in the ear of someone grieving.

Perhaps as grace said for a meal thrown together at an impromptu gathering in a makeshift shelter.

Perhaps as a concert, a celebration of shared humanity with stories and songs and smiles and cries and cheers and howls and every noise that is appropriate at a gathering that is brave and raw and honest yet unsure in some ways about its own identity.

A concert? Yes. A liturgy? Perhaps. A prayer? A rite of passage?

In the midst of disaster and pain and grief and loss and anger, what does prayer sound like?

Like the sound wave that cannot be seen, we witness these prayers in the movement of others.

We see the prayerful preparation of emergency accommodation, of impromptu meals.
We see the prayers of pain and hope in rituals and rites.
We see the prayers of comfort in bouquets and candles.

We may not always recognise it through the noise and disquiet, but it is there, playing out across our television screens, amongst us in stadiums and in kirks, whispering in homes and echoing through hallways.

Prayer does not always start when we choose.

It may not always crescendo to shouts of hallelujah and songs of praise, but when the invisible is made visible, the vibrations are felt far and wide.

Written by PHILL MELLSTROM

PRAYER NOTES

Call and response

*Repentance means turning toward other human beings,
our own flesh and blood, whenever they're oppressed, hungry,
or imprisoned; it means acting with compassion instead of
indifference.*

~ Sara Miles, from *City of God: Faith in the Streets* ~

God has a human face; that of a brown-eyed, brown-faced, Palestinian Jew who faced asylum, homelessness, prejudice, imprisonment and execution 2000 years ago. Jesus, the revelation of God, promised that God would continue to be with us through the power of the Holy Spirit (John 14:26), in bread and wine (Luke 22:19–20) and amongst the excluded and marginalised (Matthew 25:31 ff).

When we encounter some of the great 'social evils' of our day – such as hunger, violence, loneliness, climate change, forced migration and poor health – we encounter them not simply as structural injustices, but as people who have human faces. When we choose to look and listen, to search out, they have names. For me, they are people called Caroline, Jean, Maqsood and William. They are people who inspire me and help me to understand more clearly what is wrong in our world. They also help me to know Jesus; they deepen my faith, strengthen my resolve and help me to pray.

Sometimes the call to pray for those afflicted by poverty and injustice sounds and feels like a reverse shopping list. So, for example: 'Lord, we pray for the poor, for the homeless, for asylum seekers and refugees, and for those whose lives are blighted by violence.' Of course, there is nothing wrong with such prayer, individual and corporate, but we need to find ways, if possible, to give it added colour, depth and spirit. Our prayer life, our commitment to the present and coming reign of God, is transformed when our prayers for the world have real names.

One of the earliest books I read about prayer described praying as the Christian's vital breath. Although I now can't remember the name of the book (or the author), the image and sound have stuck with me – prayer is that process of inhaling and exhaling. It is as foundational to faith as breathing is to life. This helps us to see that prayer is not a topping or a tailing of what we do (or don't do) in our pursuit of justice; it is an integral part of justice-building. Pursuing justice is not distinct from prayer; it is part of prayer: 'Thy kingdom come, Your will be done, on earth as it is in heaven.'

During the First Gulf War, the congregation I was part of decided to host a nightly service to pray for peace for as long as the conflict continued. It was led by people from all the different churches in the town. We had no idea how long it would be necessary and certainly no sense of how many people might come along. People came with different motives. Some were avowed pacifists. Many others came because their sons were frontline soldiers serving in the region and they desperately wanted them home safely. Every night for eight weeks, 20, 30 and occasionally as many as 50 people gathered to pray for peace. Perhaps even more interesting, our prayers led us to do more. A group of people started meeting in the church hall before and after the service making up 'peace boxes', containing toiletries, small gifts and handwritten cards for those who were being displaced by the conflict. One night, the mother of Bobbie, a young man who had been deployed to the region, read a letter from him telling how grateful the children he had met were for our gifts. Imperfect though our words and actions might have been, our prayers, nonetheless, had a human face.

Amidst the sounds, sights and smells of injustice – the cry of those who struggle against poverty, the shocking sight of a young boy's body washed up on a Mediterranean beach, the stench of an open sewer running past people's homes – we often find ourselves thrown towards prayer. And as we do so, we hear ourselves listening to the grief and sadness of God.

In that place, that place of prayerful listening, we are renewed and invigorated for the prayer-filled actions that flow.

There was a time when the activist in me believed that the movement to prayer constituted escapism. We don't know what to do (or we know what to do but it is too hard), so we choose to pray instead. Two things have changed my heart about this. The first is the passionate prayers and resilient faith of those who face injustice. The second is the reality that prayer and action are not separate entities; they are the sound of the inward and outward breath of the Christian.

Written by MARTIN JOHNSTONE

PRAYER NOTES

Doppler effect

How long, O Lord?
  Will You forget me forever?

~ Psalm 13:1 ~

These words, associated with David, were written in order to express his sense of abandonment to God. This is not a sentiment popular among Christians today who believe that 'God is always near me,' and if God is not, then there is something wrong with me.

We can see how sacred words that would be heartfelt when first uttered, tend to be avoided by later generations of people who, failing to understand the confusing realities of life for biblical characters, instead think that the 'true believer' should never doubt God's presence. However, where true believers of today find themselves the objects of endless persecution, rather than enjoying lives of relative ease, these words might find renewed resonance.

Prayers and sacred texts change their significance as they move across cultures and centuries. In the mid 19th century, when urban and rural areas witnessed high rates of childhood mortality, this prayer had a particular poignancy:

Now I lay me down to sleep,
I pray the Lord my soul to keep.
If I should die before I wake,
I pray the Lord my soul to take.

~ Traditional children's prayer ~

But in today's society, where infant mortality is a fraction of what it was in Victorian times, is this the kind of devotional text we should be asking children to pray? Associated with such prayers are hymn texts from the same era depicting heaven as a place where:

There with happy children
robed in snowy white,
I will see my saviour
in that world so bright.

~ Fanny Crosby (Francis van Alstyne) (1820–1915) ~

For children in 19th-century industrial Britain, these images of
a 'happy land' to which they might imminently depart might
have been consoling; for children today, however, such images
could be spiritually damaging, given that their first experience
of death is far more likely to be that of a grandparent or older
relative rather than a sibling.

When asked what they are most apprehensive about today,
children often bring up fears such as mum and dad splitting up,
or a fear of strangers, or a fear that the world is becoming
dangerous because of ecological uncertainty. Among teenagers,
concerns expressed are a fear of failure at school, or
disappointment with their looks, or a fear of loneliness despite
social media connections.

The children's songs that deal with such contemporary realities
are relatively few. Fischy Music (based in Edinburgh) offer
good resources in this regard. For example, in one of their
songs, the first verse offers children a much-needed
consolation should their personal or family circumstances take
a turn for the worse.

When I'm feeling sad, I can call out to Him.
When it hurts inside, he feels every tear.
When no one understands just what I'm thinking
*   Jesus, he's always there,*
*   he's always there.*

~ Stephen Fischbacher (1960) (CH4, hymn 569) ~

There is one recent strand of popular devotional material that
finds its root in times long past. During the 19th century,
Alexander Carmichael began to collect poems and prayers
from Gaelic-speaking people in the highlands and islands of

Scotland. He was concerned that, as the Gaelic language was superseded by English, unique spiritual insights and ever-pertinent wisdom might be lost.

The poems, sayings, songs and prayers were collected and published in translation as *Carmina Gadelica* – 'Songs of the Gaels'. In them, we find models for prayer in which God is addressed not just in a quiet moment at the beginning or ending of the day, but at all times and in all places. There are prayers for everything from breastfeeding a baby to sending cattle into the pasture. There are prayers for setting out on a sea journey and against people who have evil intentions. Here is a prayer for consecrating woven cloth:

> *May the man of this clothing never be wounded,*
> *may torn he never be;*
> *what time he goes into battle or combat,*
> *may the sanctuary shield of the Lord be his.*
>
> ~ *Carmina Gadelica* by Alexander Carmichael (Floris Books) ~

These texts are both authentic and charming, but the icons of island spirituality from centuries back cannot be expected to fulfil the devotional needs of urban dwellers today.

A parent, for example, might want to say a prayer for their children as they see them off to school. A carer might say a prayer for those in their charge who are losing their mental clarity. An executive might have a prayer to say before a board meeting.

Here, then, is an example of a modern-day equivalent that enables an individual, on waking, to ponder on what lies ahead in the day and offer their daily activities for God's blessing.

> *God bless to me today*
> *my eyes and my seeing,*
> *my ears and my hearing,*
> *my lips and my speaking.*

God bless to me today
  my hands and my holding,
  my feet and my moving,
  my body and my health.

God bless to me today
  my mind and my thinking,
  my heart and my loving,
  my soul and my believing.

~ © WGRG The Iona Community ~

We can see how the fertile store of prayers from previous generations offer models for our age. Their inspiration allows us to develop a treasury of short prayers appropriate to the activities of daily life, to be prayed while carrying out the activity. In this way, the practice – if not the words – of the past can greatly enrich and enliven the prayer of people today.

Written by JOHN BELL

Harmony

Let the nations be glad and sing for joy,
for You judge the peoples with equity
and guide the nations upon earth.
Let the peoples praise You, O God;
let all the peoples praise You.

~ Psalm 67:4–5 ~

Psalm 67 speaks about the nations of the earth being glad and singing for joy together. Isn't it interesting that the kingdom of God isn't described as one culturally homogenous nation, but rather consists of people from every tribe and tongue and nation. Each tongue will have a different style of speaking, praying and singing, and yet we are still described as the kingdom of God. Let's then consider how the Church can be in harmony through our sung worship and prayers.

Harmony is best experienced not when several notes are played at the same time on the same instrument, but when notes are played together on several different instruments. The variety in timbre and texture of the instruments blends to create a richer sound. In Church, we have a variety of voices that all bring their unique timbre and texture. The challenge is not to be in discord, but rather choose to serve our neighbour in love to create a rich harmony.

However, do we as the local church fully understand who our neighbours are? In my local parish church in north east Glasgow, we long to be in harmony rather than dissonance with our neighbours. What then is our church to look like in its place within society and as a part of the culture? To have a theology of loving our neighbour is to have a mode of interaction with culture, to value what they value, and to take a position of loving humility. When someone walks into church who has never been in church before, will they feel like they can join in the worship?

For many, the hymns and songs will be unfamiliar and the tunes often difficult to pick up. We had to ask ourselves as a church how we could let the people of north east Glasgow praise God together in harmony with one another. We decided to use songs that are similar to a Scottish folk music style, as this is something found within the culture in Scotland, and so people who may never have been to church before can pick this up more easily. For example, at a recent holiday club service, it was encouraging to see nearly everyone singing *For All That You Have Done* (by the band Rend Collective) to the tune of *Auld Lang Syne*; this service included many who had never previously been to church. In this way neighbours were in harmony with one another.

On occasion, newcomers to our church have an idea that in Christian culture, you are only considered to be holy if you speak eloquently and sing excellently. Yet worshipping God sincerely doesn't mean we do an impression of what we think Christian culture is, as the Bible never mentions singing excellently! Rather, we encourage everyone to come to God as they were made, with their own unique accent, voice and choice of words, as equal children of God.

To this end, we often sing a version Psalm 136, *Give Thanks To God*; within it, there is space for people to spontaneously sing or pray out a line in their own words, with all of us then joining in.

> (Individual:) *Thanks, Lord, for helping me with that frustrating situation at work.*
>
> (All together:) *His never-ending love is steadfast and sure.*
>
> (Individual:) *I really couldn't have made it through this week without You.*
>
> (All together:) *Give thanks to God, for He is good.*

To sing in harmony with one another is to recognise that our neighbour may not be going through the same life situation as us, yet we honour them by singing with them about the hard things in their lives. As the Book of Psalms is the word of God, alive and active, it gives us individually and corporately a voice, words or a language to express our emotions.

If in our services we have a wide range of songs expressing varied emotions, then some will express how we currently feel and some won't. For example, Psalm 13 asks, 'How long will anxious thoughts prevail? My heart has sorrow day by day,' which may or may not be how we are feeling. Singing this song in harmony with others helps us to appreciate and love our neighbour who does have anxious thoughts; it also gives us a song for when we may have such thoughts in the future.

Harmony in church is an act of humility: letting other voices be equally heard in song and prayer. My prayer is that our church family of different voices will be united in harmonious worship to God, and in love for God and one another.

Written by PETE CROCKETT

www.petecrockett.com/psalms-for-all-folk

PRAYER NOTES

Dissonance

Sae come aa ye at hame wi freedom
Never heed whit the houdies croak for Doom
In yer hoos aa the bairns o Adam
Will find breid, barley-bree an paintit rooms.

~ *Freedom Come-All-Ye*
© Hamish Henderson 1960 ~

A desire to end inequality and give every person the best possible chance in life was what drew me into active politics as a teenager in the Scottish Borders; it was what drove me as an MSP, and it is what still drives me today as a Christian in 21st-century Scotland. Growing up in the Borders, the thought that I would one day be the first woman elected to a Scottish Parliament couldn't have been further from my mind. Politics was for someone else, not a mill-worker's daughter from Jedburgh. Yet, in the end, it was where God wanted me to serve for 12 years.

To the external eye, politics is marked by dissonance, by argument and tension – oftentimes between politicians, sometimes between politicians and special-interest groups, and occasionally even between politicians and constituents who challenge them. Politicians can be downright rude and nasty to each other – in the debating chamber, in the press and sometimes in person. It's a world where theology and ideology are not always easy bedfellows. So why then, as a Christian, would I want throw to myself into this hostile and challenging life?

It came without doubt from my upbringing, where politics and church ran side by side. The Jesus I knew was a man who cared deeply about the poor, the marginalised, the unloved – not in a 'there, there' kind of way, but in a dynamic, active way, tackling issues head on. The Bible shows us that we are not to be passive observers but to be active participants in the world around us; to look beyond our own walls and see a world in need, as Jesus did, and to do something about it.

And so, after years as a youth worker and trade union activist, I entered Parliament, not really prepared for what was to come. That heady excitement of the opening of the Scottish Parliament in July 1999 had almost disappeared by September. It was a time of real conflict and tension. Just days before Christmas that same year, a gas explosion in my own constituency that claimed the lives of a young family had me facing a situation that nothing can really prepare you for. It was this event that made me so conscious of my need for prayer, not only to support a grieving family but also to seek guidance as to how best to effect change to ensure that no one else faced a similar situation.

Throughout my time in Parliament, whether in big moral debates or in the bread and butter of constituency life, I had to work out how to balance my Christian values when they were in conflict with the views of my party or my constituents. The most obvious and public example was the repeal of Clause 28 (intentionally promoting homosexuality in schools) and the huge campaign – run mainly by Christians – to block its repeal. My party wanted to repeal the act; however, many Christian constituents didn't – and I found myself caught in the middle. Eventually, it was my experience as a youth worker that convinced me that we had to be able to support young people struggling with issues of sexuality to feel loved, valued and accepted.

It was a hard time in Scottish politics, but what I found out quite quickly was that politicians of all hues and all parties face the same struggles. By meeting together and praying with each other, we could support each other, even when we were on opposite sides of a debate. In the most difficult days and debates, it was those times of prayer early in the morning that saw me through – that and knowing that there were people outside the Parliament every day praying for my colleagues and me. Perhaps the most visible reminder of that was a group of folk who came every week and sat in the public gallery wearing red, not as a political statement, but as a visual reminder that they were remembering the Parliament and its members in prayer. They have never missed a week. That commitment to praying for those in 'high positions', as Paul puts it in 1 Timothy 2:2, was a huge encouragement to people in the Parliament of all faiths and none. Knowing that the institution and everyone who was part of it was valued, cared for – and prayed for – when sometimes it didn't feel that way, helped to keep us focused on the job.

We are urged to uphold politicians prayerfully, in 'supplications, prayers, intercessions, and thanksgivings'. By getting to know our local politicians, meeting with them, saying 'hello' when we bump into them in the supermarket – these simple acts can encourage them and let them know that they are being prayed for. I know it certainly helped and encouraged me.

The Bible is not short of examples of how we should turn prayer into action, and nowhere more so than in the Beatitudes. As we read scripture and allow prayer to turn to action, we might be inspired to contact our representatives, write letters, lobby or even take part in a protest, so that communal decisions can be informed and touched by prayer. Through prayer, the dissonance of politics can be transformed into the harmony of resolution and positive action for the common good.

Written by KAREN GILLON

PRAYER NOTES

Tumult

When my soul is in the dumps, I rehearse
*   everything I know of You,*
From Jordan depths to Hermon heights,
*   including Mount Mizar.*
Chaos calls to chaos,
*   to the tune of whitewater rapids.*
Your breaking surf, Your thundering breakers
*   crash and crush me.*

~ Psalm 42:6–7 (The Message) ~

Our house is six miles from the sea, yet on a stormy night you can hear the stones thundering at Bay of Skaill, crashing over one another in the relentless violence of the surf. The noise is awe inspiring and when it is over, there is silence and a thick crust of salt on the windows.

How do we pray in the midst of storms? How do we give voice to inner turmoil? In the tumult of our crises, prayer can erupt spontaneously – 'God, help me now!' – or it can die, still half formed on our lips.

There is a long and rich tradition of prayer in the midst of mental distress – the Psalms are ancient and eloquent testimony to this – but like any tradition, if it is not nourished and passed on, it becomes remote and inaccessible. How to give voice to distress is especially difficult when it is the competing voices that are causing the distress.

Up to a quarter of the population have experienced auditory hallucinations – hearing voices. They can be helpful and healthy but are also a feature of mental illness, particularly schizophrenia, manic depression and psychosis. Voices can often start after a traumatic event, especially amongst children, and there can be such stigma associated with it that many become isolated and withdrawn. Health professionals used to distract people from talking about voices, believing that discussing them made their grip stronger, but it is now felt that articulating and befriending these voices is an important part of coping and recovery.

Listening and giving voice, two essential components of prayer, also happen to be two essential components of dealing with mental illness. Whether it is to ourselves or to one another, listening and giving voice are crucial to our wellbeing.

Yet here too there are challenges. When in anguish, it is hard to listen and hard to give voice. The noise of competing voices can be deafening. The silence, too, can be deafening. God can feel absent, far removed from us. God can also appear all too present in the midst of turmoil, close at hand, though not resolving the cause of our despair. Sometimes it is hard to know which is more disturbing.

An analogy that can be helpful is that of standing waves, a physical phenomenon caused by interference between two waves travelling in opposite directions. In acoustics, it results in fixed points where sound is amplified and others where it is cancelled out. The noise of competing voices can be like this – at points it is overwhelming in intensity and at other points it creates a void of silence: points of terrifying intimacy with God and points of terrifying isolation from God. Each needs to be acknowledged and befriended through prayer, even when that prayer is a wordless silence of clinging on by our fingernails.

Despair contains within it the deeply felt lie of hopeless abandonment. Distraction, pretence, papering over the cracks – these do little to help. Acknowledging the strength of what is felt is important – but in prayer we acknowledge that strength and at the same time acknowledge a greater strength, which we call God. Murderous rage, intense distress, overwhelming sadness – these emotions have the power to destroy us and others. Prayer offers a safety valve of venting these to God, who is big enough both to hear us and to help us, to listen and give voice, even if such care-filled attention rarely offers easy or immediate solutions.

The Psalms are full of people giving voice to destructive emotions, outlining exactly what it is that God should be doing and isn't, and often then acknowledging that God may have another plan – but it had better work out!

One of the many mysteries of faith is that there is no way to escape extremes of experience, that God does not eliminate the valleys of the shadow of death but instead gifts us the courage and love we need to walk through them.

I have a storm-tumbled stone from Bay of Skaill in my pocket. It is smooth and comforting to hold, and in times of distress I have clung to it as if to God's very self. Gripping it is as much as I can pray sometimes, yet it is perhaps my most articulate prayer – I won't let go.

Written by DAVID MCNEISH

PRAYER NOTES

Silence

'And when you pray, do not keep on babbling like pagans,
for they think they will be heard because of their many words.'

~ Matthew 6:7 (NIV) ~

The 19th-century Scottish poet and hymn writer, James
Montgomery, begins his hymn on prayer with this stanza:

Prayer is the soul's sincere desire,
uttered or unexpressed;
the motion of a hidden fire
that trembles in the breast.

If there is a naturalness to prayer, the 'soul's sincere desire',
why do we concentrate on the 'uttered' part and struggle with
'unexpressed' prayers? In Romans 8:26, Paul says:

Likewise the Spirit helps us in our weakness; for we do
not know how to pray as we ought, but that very Spirit
intercedes with sighs too deep for words.

These 'sighs too deep for words' can also be our prayers.
Mahatma Gandhi tells us:

Prayer is not asking. It is a longing of the soul. It is the
daily admission of one's weakness.

There is often no way to express our deep longings. But when
we believe praying is only about words, then what is
'unexpressed' in us is considered valueless. 'Our prayers are
dry,' we cry, and feel we have failed.

I helped care for John Levering when he was dying. 'There are
times,' this profoundly spiritual man told me, 'when I have no
words to bring me close to God in prayer. But I do not despair.
For I know many people will be praying, not only *for* me, but
will be *praying my prayers for me*. In my wordless silences,
my prayers will yet be heard.'

Weighed down by the burden of getting the words right, we can miss the longings of our soul. Silence for Gandhi and John Levering wasn't failure, but being open to a deep awareness of the longings within them, which can lead to true communion with God.

Jesus taught His disciples that when prayers are 'vain repetitions' and we are 'babbling like pagans', then they have no value. Our words have lost their heart. Better then, suggests John Bunyan, to have a 'heart without words than to have words without a heart', and be truly at one with God.

In my 15 years as a hospice chaplain, there were many times when I could find no words for an appropriate prayer. People regularly looked to me for a spiritual gem. If *they* couldn't find the words, they expected me to do it for them. On too many occasions I took the wrong path. I sought words in the face of trauma when there were none. I should have given more time to silence and let communion with God be enough.

The French novelist, Georges Bernanos wrote in his *Journal d'un curé de campagne* ('The Diary of a Country Priest') that 'The wish for prayer is prayer itself'.

A chaplain in an AIDS hospice told me that, after the death of a young woman whom the team had got very close to, he'd arrived at work to find that the 'last offices' were underway. In the patient's room, he found three nurses continuing to care for the young woman as tenderly in death as they had in life. They were all in tears, and it wasn't long before the chaplain was crying too. 'I had nothing to say,' he told me. 'So after I'd given each of them a hug, I let them get on with their work.' When the 'last offices' were done, one of the nurses said, 'I think she should be anointed, Father Terry.' An Anglican chaplain was familiar enough with the ritual. 'But,' he recounted, 'I had no oil or prayer book. How could I do justice to this?' But, drawing his finger across his tear-stained cheek, he anointed the young woman on the forehead with the sign of the cross. And, one by one, the three nurses did the same, anointing their friend with their own tears. No words were spoken. Yet that room of death had been transformed into a cathedral of prayer.

The wish for prayer was prayer itself. 'If any words had been spoken,' Terry said, 'we would have compromised the healing touch of God which was clear to everyone in that room.'

In *Hamlet*, Shakespeare has King Claudius say,

> *My words fly up, my thoughts remain below:*
> *Words without thoughts never to heaven go.*

~ Shakespeare, *Hamlet*, Act 3, Scene 3 ~

If the words of our prayers fly up and there is no thought to them, if they are empty of meaning, like the 'vain repetition' or 'babbling' to which Jesus refers, then they will count for nothing. Words can be a barrier to a healing relationship with God. But if we break down that barrier and allow our true yearnings to be communicated in silence, then our prayers will rise to heaven indeed.

> *In the solitude of my silence I was close to You, my God,*
> *For I knew, in quiet wordlessness,*
> *The truth of my longings, the unspoken yearnings of my soul.*
> *God of the silent times, I am speaking with You now.*

Written by TOM GORDON

PRAYER NOTES

Sound barrier

When you're between a rock and a hard place,
it won't be a dead end –
Because I am God, your personal God.

~ Isaiah 43:2–3 (The Message) ~

Oyster-catchers come and go, camouflaging their eggs
amongst the pebbles that meet the paths. There are walking
groups that regularly provide the opportunity for women in
custody to benefit from fresh air, exercise and some sense of
space. Recently, stones have been laid to reveal the Latin
phrase *Dum spiro spero,* with a plaque handily providing the
translation: 'While I breathe I hope.' It makes a difference that
there are wide open spaces at HMP&YOI Cornton Vale. The
award-winning Gardens Team makes creative expression
through planting colourful flowers and sculpting the landscape.

Sometimes, when people meet for prayer or worship in The
Sanctuary, the sounds of birds can be heard or the sounds of
people going about, of cars and, some have said even, of the
River Forth - reminders of life and of God's sustaining care;
the sounds of people interacting, having conversations,
'getting on with it', sometimes laughter and radios playing,
and exercise.

Other noises are here also: sometimes the sounds of disturbed
people shouting because it is what they are driven to do by the
mental ill-health that besets them. Notwithstanding the work of
prison staff, nurses, doctors, psychologists, chaplains and
others, people have been traumatised so deeply by life that
calm eludes them. Overwhelmed by the pressure of bad
memories, regret and trauma, the pain of loss or separation,
some people express confusion; the sounds of tears falling in
sadness, anxiety or rage. Some raise their voices – the tonal
changes when people express their emotions are recognised –
giving vent to the pressure that can no longer be held in.

These words of Isaiah are often shared:

> *Don't be afraid, I've redeemed you.*
> *I've called your name. You're mine.*
> *When you're in over your head, I'll be there with you.*
> *When you're in rough waters, you will not go down.*
> *When you're between a rock and a hard place,*
> *it won't be a dead end –*
> *Because I am God, your personal God,*
> *The Holy of Israel, your Saviour.*

~ Isaiah 43:2–3 (The Message) ~

Recently, the sounds of a person talking rapidly remained with me. So bothered was she, that her words rushed out in staccato, sounding like a machine gun, until in it all, somewhere, she asked: 'Can we say a prayer?' And we did, and there was calm, peaceful, blissful, for a while, at least.

Here are quieter times, such as when people come to The Sanctuary to light a candle to pray for someone or to remember someone. Time is taken to be still, to experience silence, to gain strength to better meet the rest of the day. Sound can be like a barrier, in the way of wellbeing, but when that sound barrier is broken, in the still small quiet moments, the love of the God who is with us in all circumstances becomes apparent again and there is hope and some healing.

Sometimes the sound barrier is not broken. Prayer is often associated with quiet, but if there is no quiet, there can still be prayer! The sounds can be absorbed and offered to God; perhaps they will lead us to pray more meaningfully for our neighbours on their journey, or for ourselves.

We made paper boats last Sunday.

The reading was about Jesus being woken from His sleep in the back of a boat by the shouts of His friends asking was it nothing to Him that they would drown? And we chatted about how Jesus was there in the storm (no fair-weather friend is He) and how, when it's like a maelstrom and we are on the edge, it makes a difference to bring our anxious thoughts, our inner storms, to Jesus. We noted that Jesus can bring calm into the most difficult of situations. When people laid their paper boats on the Communion table, they offered a prayer for others experiencing challenging times, or for themselves.

Music has a special place. People playing the Taiko drums often experience strong emotions through the sound of the drum. Many report feeling soothed, while others feel energised and lighter. Some take the chance to learn the guitar. Then there are occasional evening singalongs. Singing groups have been supported by members of the community who love to sing and see the benefits that singing brings: lifting the spirits and creating wellbeing, affirming talents and building community.

At Sunday worship in Cornton Vale, the style is participative. Questions are welcomed and oft-times the reflection has to be abandoned for something totally different but which speaks more directly to the issues people are wrestling with inside or outside.

The sounds of this custodial environment are many.

They are at times discordant but there are softer notes, grace notes too. Prayer here, like the Psalms, attempts to embrace it all and offer it to the God who hears us.

Written by BILL TAYLOR

PRAYER NOTES

Echo

What we did as we climbed, and what we talked of
Matters not much, nor to what it led...
It filled but a minute. But was there ever
A time of such quality, since or before,
In that hill's story ? ...
But what they record in colour and cast
Is—that we two passed.

~ Thomas Hardy, from 'At Castle Boterel' ~

Feeling the wind about us, we stood outside the stone buildings of the Camas Centre on Mull in the early part of the day, soothed by the lapping of the sea near our feet. The silence was broken by shouting each of our names towards the quarry opposite. Each of us individually could feel the power of who we were out there in the air and then in the rebound of our name echoing back towards us. We could claim our name, but as it resounded, each name took on a life of its own.

In their song, 'Streets of Edinburgh', The Proclaimers tell of the ghosts and stories of a time in our lives that have a power over us. Just walking down a street can open up the vault of memories inside us, memories that can grip us and hold us fast in that time and space, but which can also catapult us to a new place, one that strengthens us and reminds us of who we are and who we can be.

We thought a lot about the lives of Castlemilk East and Castlemilk West at the time of our union into Castlemilk Parish Church in Glasgow. As a congregation, we paused to take time to pray, bringing forth all the stories of prayers made, answered and unanswered. We couldn't help but see that we were part of the answers to the prayers made by many who were no longer around. There was a sense of a faithful community of God's people urging us onwards in our faithful lives that would take us to somewhere they were never to see.

As part of our endings to each congregation, we created a touching point with our prayerful past by making small wooden crosses from the pews from Castlemilk East and wooden hearts from the pews of Castlemilk West, which everyone could take home. The power of a little piece of the place we were letting go of that we could have in our own homes, made a connection to the place and people we loved.

The stories that came out at these times of change – the closure of Castlemilk East, the union of the two congregations, the closure of Castlemilk West and the opening of our new church building – were a wonderful uncovering of the life of faith that individuals and the congregations each held. There were stories of weddings and baptisms, of burnt-out cars, of herding of non-churchgoers to participate; there were tales of talent shows and fayres, of dancing and baking; and there were psalms and laments of pain and death, telling of the sharpness of difficult relationships and the loss of valued ones. Among all of the tales was a thread woven of God and the power and depth of relationship upheld through song and story and prayer.

In our new building, all of these prayers and stories from the past are carved into the furniture in our sanctuary. We set up a woodwork project and used the wood from the pews of our former churches to make new things out of the old. Three woods were used: cedar from Castlemilk East – a traditional religious wood; Scots pine from the pews of Castlemilk West – an echo of our heritage; and oak – symbolising the strength in our union together.

Our story is about more than the echoes of the past; it is also about how each of us in the present hears them and responds to them. We invited local people to be involved in the making of the church furniture, connecting them to the people of the past and writing themselves into the story of now. They will forever be connected to people they have never met, and are now part of the echoes of the beginnings of this new chapter in the life of the church in Castlemilk.

One of the hardest things to let go of is the echo of love and laughter – and the silence that follows it – that holds you in the deepest, most sacred moments of your life. In those ending moments, the final weekends in each of those churches, there was an atmosphere of sacred bonds being severed forever. To deny that this was painful would be to ignore the reality that change brings with it grief – which does not end when you walk away or start something new. But the comfort came from the echoing of the prayers of those who had died or moved on with their lives, and the power those prayers still held. The legacies of each one gave power to what was yet to come – they were still part of that unfolding story.

Written by SARAH BROWN

PRAYER NOTES

Cry

A voice out of the land –
animal, vegetable, mineral –
'The pain, the beauty – Why, why, why?
Tell me the truth, give me
understanding.'

$\sim$ R.S. Thomas, from 'Aim' $\sim$

Answer me, O Lord!

It echoes around the incense-filled sanctuary.

Answer me, O Lord!

Once more, this desperate plea in Arabic: *istajibni ya rabb.*

Answer me, O Lord!

These lines of the liturgy cut through the sensory overload of
my first visit to Bethlehem's Syriac Orthodox Church. The
repetition certainly helped, as did the plaintive, almost tortured
oriental melody and the pointed silences between each
utterance. But the longer I dwelt with that community, the
more intensely these lines affected me. The connection of these
cries to Syriac and Palestinian experience – the focus of my
research there – gave them ever increasing force. Sometimes
they were rendered in Arabic, sometimes in the ancient
liturgical language of Syriac Aramaic that, plausibly, Jesus
Himself would have understood.

istajibni ya rabb! anin moryo!
Answer me, O Lord!

For Syriac Christians in the West Bank, the hardships of
occupation and the displacements of the past century are
simply a modern episode of trauma among countless upheavals
that punctuate their ancient story. Syriac Orthodox Christians
were excluded by the Council of Chalcedon in 451; became
victims of both the Western Christendom Crusades and the

slaughters of the Mongol Khans; and above all, suffered the genocide of 1915, in which they were uprooted wholesale from south-east Turkey alongside Armenians and Greeks. They simply call this terrible act 'the Sword' or *seyfo*.

In recent years, another heartland of Syriac Christianity, northern Iraq, experienced almost total 'cleansing' of Christians, although happily there are now some signs of a fragile restoration. Still, there is no retelling of the Syriac Christian story that doesn't include episodes of violent displacement and genocide. The future is far from certain.

Answer me, O Lord!

This phrase echoes dozens of biblical psalms. Three thousand years of wrestling with the God of the Promises have produced countless answers to the questions posed by these experiences of deep sorrow – and especially by the silence that so often follows. There is wisdom for us in these accumulated answers.

But the fact that the Bible and our liturgies bequeath these appeals to us, so often unresolved, tells us that there must be space for such cries in the lives of our communities. Careful attention to the implications of this may influence how we come to think of prayer itself.

The Arabic word for prayer, *salat*, comes from an Aramaic root, *sluto*, which means to slope or incline. Prayer is not only our words but our posture before God, our inclination towards or leaning in to God.

Perhaps this brings to mind comforting images: the flower tending towards sunlight and receiving nourishment; the nuzzling of a cub into its mother's gentle immensity.

But how do we respond when the light is gone? When the source of our life seems absent?

Let us look at the worst crises in the contemporary Middle East, from the starving people of Yemen, to the destroyed lives of Syria. Let's look into the eyes of a refugee widow in Iraq, a child imprisoned in Gaza who cannot get the healthcare they need, a victim of domestic violence in Egypt to whom no local official will listen.

Confronted by such hardship on a daily basis we could, eventually, stop inclining, stop reaching, stop crying. Reports of children in orphanages around the world describe infants reaching a point of such neglect that they stop crying for the love and nourishment they need.

The cry, then, is an involuntary act of faith; perhaps even a sign that some hope remains, against the odds.

Voicing anguish in our communities keeps us crying when we might otherwise, on our own, give up.

Answer me, O Lord!

This, then, is a crying together. At times, we are conscious of God's presence, of God's involvement in our lives and in our world. When this is the case, others' cries – both poetic and visceral – are unsettling, and perhaps even more when silence follows.

But as part of the same body of Christ, the same household of God, our individual and communal transformation is connected to being unsettled in this way. This becomes the basis of our intercession: our ability to cry with our brothers and sisters, to place those words – whether from scripture, from our newspapers, or from the lips of people we know – in the first person, and make them our own.

This might not fix anything, yet still, just sometimes, in inhabiting this posture of crying, we may become agents of hope and healing.

The era of slaughters in south east Turkey that culminated in the *seyfo* is precisely the environment in which our forebears bore witness to the horror of their Syriac, Armenian and Greek family's suffering, heard their cries, and saw the light of Christ that God's faithful people shone in the midst of this apparent absence of God. They could not avert these historic catastrophes but, having cried with those who suffered through the darkness, they were also moved to help their dispersed Christian brothers and sisters. They helped to establish schools, hospitals and organisations that, to this day, radiate Christ's light across the region.

They were there when the flower withered, when its straining for light was met by utter darkness. But they were there too when its scattered seed began to produce green shoots that God is still bringing to fruit now.

Today, we take up their legacy. Will we also be there: in the crying, in the darkness, in the strength of their continued service, and to be a part of what God will plant and grow next?

istajibni ya rabb! anin moryo!
Answer me, O Lord!

Written by MARK CALDER

Mark Calder is the Regional Manager covering Scotland and the North of England for Embrace the Middle East, the ecumenical charity that has been partnering with Christians in the region to tackle poverty and injustice for more than 160 years. They were there to support their brothers and sisters as they faced the *seyfo*, and they are still there now. You can find out more at www.embraceme.org

Natural

The kiss of the sun for pardon,
The song of the birds for mirth,
One is nearer God's heart in a garden,
Than anywhere else on earth.

~ Dorothy Gurney, from 'God's Garden' ~

Poet and hymn writer Dorothy Gurney's oft-quoted words are easily over-sentimentalised. So too the protestations of the avid golfer that one can be just as close to God on the golf course on a Sunday morning as one is in church. That may well be true, but should we confuse the general feeling of wellbeing in an awe-inspiring place, with communion with the Creator God on an intense or meaningful level?

Nature does inspire. In the Genesis story, humanity's first experience of God, and communication with God, occurs in a garden – a garden created in an ordered way and seen by God as 'good'. There was, and is, a clear interrelatedness between creature and Creator. The very air breathed was the breath of God.

As a result of what happened in that garden, though, the relationship is changed. After an outpouring of joy at the fullness of creation comes a more strident voice associated with hardship and toil (Genesis 3:17ff). Along with the responsibility of stewarding a beautiful and productive Eden, comes confrontation on drought-devastated land, in barren wilderness and in places made waste by war. These places cry out for our prayers. Sadly, however, we children of Adam and Eve have often lost the capacity to sense the presence of Almighty God, unsure how to hear the word and will of God in the garden breeze.

In a world, indeed a universe, unimaginable to the writers of Genesis, we need, more than ever, to sense the very breath of God within and around us. We may be moved to pray to give thanks for the beauty of the created world, to express our distress at the amount of plastic waste creating havoc in our oceans and the amount of junk floating around in space; yet we remain somehow paralysed by the enormity of making a difference ourselves. How can we be more inspired and moved to action as our prayerful response to the love of our Creator God?

The ecumenical Eco Congregation movement that has blossomed in the last 16 years has provided much by way of encouragement and imagination in this sphere. With a blend of spirituality and practicality, it has helped to bring into being projects that call for us to step outside Dorothy Gurney's garden momentarily so that the essence of meaningful spiritual relationships might be shared.

Carlops is one small but very enthusiastic congregation recognised with a Gold Award from Eco Congregation Scotland. In this tiny Scottish village straddling a busy trunk road, the concept has been embraced with enthusiasm. The call has gone out to consider prayerfully every single use of natural resources.

And so, a delight in the wonder of the night sky, combined with an awareness of how much artificial light we waste, has led those who live there to eschew street lighting altogether.

In a total refurbishment of the interior of the church, eco principles informed the use of materials and systems. A sign in the loo even proclaims that it is twinned with a similar 'facility' in Matiti in Malawi. Older members who recall using a shed down the garden for this purpose value this as a thank-offering for the benefits of having a modern convenience.

During services and meetings, the outer wooden doors of the church remain open, proclaiming God's people doing what they do, whilst through the glass inner doors worshippers cannot but be aware of world's traffic roaring past.

These may seem tiny things, but what is so commendable in everything this congregation has achieved is that their small community is totally at one with them in all they do. Many villagers give their support out of a deeply held and professed Christian commitment, and this is reflected in their worship and at a personal level. An equal number simply have a sense of the 'rightness' and common sense of what is being attempted by the church and are ready to support it with enthusiasm and occasionally with financial contributions.

A telling example of this is the recent completion of a community garden linking the church and the village hall. Its symbolism is powerful, a tangible expression of the renewed connection between parts of our community, but also a demonstration of how our prayers and inward desires can shape our outer lives and our very environment.

So, while Dorothy Gurney's words still speak to us, they challenge us to listen carefully, to make the cry of the world and its people our cry.

One can imagine David alone with his sheep on a starlit night beginning to record the moving words of Psalm 8.

> *When I look at Your heavens, the work of Your fingers,*
> *the moon and the stars that You have established;*
> *what are human beings that You are mindful of them,*
> *mortals that You care for them?*

To speak to and to listen for God in any beautiful quiet place where reverence can be worn like a garment is a blessing, but it also brings responsibility. If we are in communication with God, we cannot help seeing brokenness alongside the beauty; we will hear both laughter and weeping; we may feel anger as well as joy. To be near to God's heart anywhere is to enjoy a sense of wonder and appreciation, but it also brings a challenge to make a living, prayed response that we can further share with others and creation.

Written by RACHEL DOBIE

PRAYER NOTES

Manufactured

Lord, look upon our working days,
busied in factory, office, store;
may wordless work Your name adore,
the common round spell out Your praise?

~ from a hymn by the late Ian M. Fraser (1917–2018)
(formerly Warden of Scottish Churches House) ~

Prayer is not so much careful composition as spontaneous
combustion. The prayers we speak or write are sparked in our
encounters and the circumstances of our lives. This article
considers what is characteristic about the prayer that is
engendered in the contemporary urban community, where
people gather to share their giftedness with each other, to do
together what cannot be done individually: to create, produce,
manufacture, serve, care, discover, regulate, govern, celebrate.
What is the distinctive sound of the prayer that arises from
the city?

The city itself prays

Just as creation 'groans and travails', the urban community
emits its cacophony of sounds, which themselves carry embryo
prayers: the jagged rejoicing that spills from the pubs at the
end of the working day; the clatter of machinery as skills are
offered; the peal of the ambulance siren reminding of the
tenuous nature of human life and health; the raucous demand
for justice in the slogans of demonstrators; the muted lament
rising from the funeral procession or the silent witness of
flowers at the site of a disaster; the welcoming hubbub of
hospitality in foodbank or house of refuge; the eureka shout
when something falls into place or a new discovery is made;
the cry of betrayal at broken trust; the shout of anger at the
oppression of the less powerful; the roar of the terrorist bomb
that intensifies the call for reconciliation; the street cries of
market traders offering and celebrating the bounty of land and
sea, factory and studio; the chirp of mobiles signalling the

multiple associations that make up human community; the parliamentary orator seeking the good of the nation; the shout of warning to save or protect the vulnerable; the burst of delighted laughter at a breakthrough or when the unexpected overturns routine.

In its own way, the city praises, gives thanks, seeks forgiveness, learns, intercedes, offers, celebrates, and gives blessing.

Personal prayer in the city

From the patterns of workplace and family, and in the variety of our encounters, fragments of personal prayer emerge, taking their form from the fragmented nature of urban living. Passing glances, brief encounters, immmediately forgotten names. Things come at us from all directions, different demands, competing opportunities. We overhear snatched phrases from the corridor, the next street, across the restaurant, the sudden raised voice, frustratingly incomplete. Our prayers, likewise, are fleeting, like light glancing off the gleaming skyscraper. Although undeveloped and tangential, they may be real and deeply felt and, in the eye of God, complete, just as when the light catches the scratches in the glass of a window, turning them into perfect circles.

Such embryo prayers may take root and grow. Our Sunday praises are enriched by the mute thank you when we find satisfaction in our skills; the anticipation as the end of the working day is signalled or a new day begins; the joy in relationships with colleagues; the loving word or gesture that brings the relief of being accepted; the stirring of the spirit at a performance or an exhibition.

Likewise, our corporate confessions and intercessions are given body by fleeting 'moments of truth' in the preceding week when we are forced to accept reality: the demands to which we do not feel equal; frustration at a setback; emptiness after a difficult encounter; unease at the compromises in which we are implicated in pursuit of a higher – or more profitable –

goal; shame at the slanders in which we have shared; despair over more news of inhumanity and injustice; the mistakes we make and our wish that we could live the moment again; bullying or abuse that destroys one's self belief; sorrow at a lost love; the times when we cry: 'I can't do this', or even, 'Why have You forsaken me?'

In the city we find Christ praying for us and with us

At the very heart of 'the trivial round, the common task', scripture comes alive as comfort or challenge:

> *'The voice of the Lord cries to the city ... what does the Lord require of you but to do justice, and to love kindness, and to walk humbly with Your God?'*
> (Micah 6:9 & 8)

> *'This is my prayer, that your love may overflow more and more with knowledge and full insight to help you to determine what is best, so that on the day of Christ you may be pure and blameless'* (Philippians 1:9–10)

> *'My grace is sufficient for you'* (2 Corinthians 12:9)

Scattered through the day are strands of that 'sufficient grace', confirming and strengthening, as Christ speaks in the voices and actions of those we meet: in the unexpected gesture of affirmation or word of love; the unlooked-for act of service; something new or different happening. Our failures are met with forgiveness, our mistakes turned to new opportunities.

> *Risen Lord, shall still our city*
> *be the city of despair?*
> *Come today, our Judge, our Glory,*
> *be its name 'The Lord is there'.*

> ~ from the hymn 'All who love and serve your city',
> by Erik Routley (1917–82)

Written by DOUGLAS GALBRAITH

PRAYER NOTES

Acknowledgements

The 52 chapters of *Pray Now* 'Together We Pray' were
written by: Fyfe Blair, Derek Browning, James Cathcart,
Adam Dillon, Sally Foster-Fulton, Ruth Harvey, Tina Kemp,
Jo Love, David Lunan, Scott McKenna, Scott McRoberts,
MaryAnn Rennie, Jock Stein, Lezley Stewart and
Jenny Williams.

Headline scripture quotations are taken from the New Revised
Standard Version, © 1989 Division of Christian Education of
the National Council of Churches of Christ in the United States
of America, published by Oxford University Press.

With special thanks to Phill Mellstrom, Felicity Burrows,
Hugh Hillyard-Parker and Rosamund Connelly for their work
in preparing the final manuscript.

Lightning Source UK Ltd.
Milton Keynes UK
UKHW031032291118
333186UK00003B/271/P